Adulting Well: Utilizing the Theories and Strategies of Dialectical Behavioral Therapy

ALEXANDRIA FIELDS MSW, LISW-S

ISBN: 978-1-7366554-0-5

DEDICATION

With my whole heart, I dedicate this book to my three daughters. I hope that adulting is an easier task for them than it was for me!

CONTENTS

ACKNOWLEDGMENTS

I could not have made it through the publishing of this book without the support of my husband. I must also thank my DBT team as they have taught me, shaped me, and kept me accountable to the skills I present in this text and without them, I wouldn't be the therapist that I am today.

Preface

This is not the type of book that you read in one week. This is not the type of book that you read once. This is also not the type of book that you keep in pristine condition! *Adulting Well* is a book of "life hacks" that you can apply daily if you want to improve your ability to delay instant gratification urges in an effort to achieve your long-term goals. I suggest that with this book, you purchase a journal and some nice pens (confession: I am a school supply addict!). I encourage you to read no more than one chapter a month and work that month on applying the strategies over and over to achieve mastery. I encourage you to re-read the same chapter during that month instead of moving on to the next chapter! I encourage you to write in this book… highlight that which stands out to you and dog-ear the important pages! I do NOT want you to leave this book in a condition that would permit Half Priced Books to buy it from you! This book is a gift to you, from me.

I wrote this book after 10 years of being a therapist and I saw a clear trend developing: the trend of avoidance and refusal to cope with pain. The generation of kids born after the mid-1980s experienced a huge parenting shift: the belief that parents should stop their children from feeling any discomfort. Gone were the days of keeping score for young soccer players, gone were punishments and limit-setting, gone were winners and losers (we all get participation trophies!), gone was a teacher's ability to fail a student, and therefore gone was a youth's ability to cope.

In the 1970s as pop-psychology was born, psychologist/researcher Martin Seligman was conducting new research on learning and ultimately discovered "learned helplessness" and its link to depression. Learned helplessness is a concept that happens when a person discovers (real or imaginary) limitations on their ability to make a change in their world. Have you ever had the thought "*Why should I even try? Each time I do, I fail.*" or "*What's the point? I never get it right.*" Those are examples of learned helplessness. I see this happening a lot with youth when they are not traditional learners…they do their best and it's never good enough! Learned helplessness helped Seligman see that that clinical depression may result from (real or perceived) lack of control over the outcome of a situation. We learn to "give up" and stop trying to influence our environment.

Unfortunately, at the same time as this research, parents were told that kids needed loads of self-esteem. This combination led to the *everyone's a winner* mentality and was the birth of the participation trophy. The unfortunate consequence has been that kids learned that nothing they did really mattered (i.e.: *"It doesn't matter if I try or don't …I'll still get a trophy"* or *"That person didn't try at all and got the same reward as I did …so why should I try?"*). Instead of self-esteem increasing, we saw learned helplessness increase. The task now, is to teach people how to struggle and persist in an effort to show themselves that they CAN cope, they CAN achieve, and that hard work DOES pay off!

The purpose of this book is just that: to teach people to experience pain, cope well, and persist through it all. Learning to tolerate short-term distress in an effort to achieve long-term goals is where self-esteem originate and can blossom into self-worth! Increased self-esteem leads to decreased depression. We need to turn our negative emotional cycles around so that our self-fulfilling prophecy is that of being competent and confident …not of being depressed and anxious failures.

Part One: Background Knowledge

1 WHO, WHAT, WHERE, WHEN, WHY?

Who (Me First):

Let's get this out of the way. Who am I and why should you care? Glad you asked! My name is Alyx Fields. My full name is Alexandria, but as a younger child it was shortened to "Alex" and I got tired of everyone assuming I was a boy …so I changed it to "Alyx" (not legally), and it stuck. A girl can only be given the racecar nametag so many times before change must be made! I am a Licensed Independent Social Worker with my supervisory designation (LISW-S), in the state of Ohio. That matters because it means that I have gotten my master's degree in the field of social work and have trained under another practicing social worker for an absurd number of hours …and then got more training so that I can now do the supervising of other social workers (also for an absurd number of hours). I have also earned my DBTC (Dialectical Behavioral Therapist Certification) designation which indicates that I have attended an impressive amount of training in Dialectical Behavioral Therapy (hereafter referred to as DBT®) and have read a heaping stack of DBT® textbooks. I am proud to report that approximately 150 of these hours were at official Behavioral Tech (parent company of DBT®) hosted trainings and approximately half of those were with Marsha Linehan (creator of DBT®) as a primary trainer. Under my direction, the DBT® Center at Compass Point in Cincinnati, Ohio has flourished and grown each year since I began to oversee it in 2012, while adhering to the strict fidelity of the model (bleh – that is enough of that).

More important than my education and training is that I am human, and I live a real life with real stress. I am eager to let you know that I will not preach anything that I have not practiced. I have attended and participated in DBT® skills classes as a participant as well as a co-facilitator and as a facilitator. I have worked (and continue to work) diligently to develop mastery in every skill taught in the DBT® Skills Training Book. I have been in the mental health field for over a decade and a DBT® therapist for 8 years in Cincinnati, Ohio. I have proudly sat on the other side of the therapy room as well, seeing therapists off and on over the last 19 years! In other words: I live it, breathe it, and because I "get it" …my clients get better. I am deeply passionate about mental health, self-care, and specifically the skills taught under the model of Dialectical Behavioral Therapy (DBT®) as they are the most "real-talk" type of skills I can give you! The skills are simple but that does not mean they are easy. There is no secret hidden agenda, simply hard work and diligence. This model so clearly outlines what is within our control and what is not – all while teaching the appropriate skills to aid in change (if it is in our control) or acceptance (if it is not).

Some people ask why I write. I have been trying hard to formulate an adequate answer. I write and blog from experience; I enjoy writing as a hobby. As I try to catch the words and phrases in my mind associated with why I write, one stands out: accountability. Naturally, I write because I enjoy helping others, I have a passion for sharing ideas that have helped me or others I have counseled, I like the mental de-cluttering that happens as I put words into sentences onto paper, but mostly, I love that it holds me accountable and keeps me passionate about being skillful in life (adulting).

I am a therapist. I am also, as it turns out, a human. A normal, fallible, prone to making mistakes human: I fall into negative self-talk, catastrophic thinking, bouts of being bummed, etc. Writing about these topics holds a mirror up to my face for me to investigate. I believe that this makes me uniquely qualified to teach you about adulting (and adulting well). Being that I am a human, an adult, a parent, a child, an employee, a citizen, etc., and that I experience stress, anger, anxiety, joy, contentment, and fear just the same as you do …I would like to think that I am relatable! I can tell you carte blanche that I am a realistic human with enough education and experience to help you change and I will show you how using real stories throughout the text. You have no reason to trust me (yet) …let me peel back the veil and show you!

I again tell you that I would never preach something that I do not (or have not) practice(d). I find that when I do not blog/teach, I do not think as logically as I could. It is apparent to me that teaching DBT® (therapy) skills classes each week is a huge BLESSING. Every week I stand in front of 10-12 people and tell them what they can do for optimal mental health; why would I ignore a message I so passionately believe in? I do not profess to be a picture of mental perfection as I do not believe that exists. Hypothetically speaking, the Suzy Sunshine's of the world likely have more baggage to unpack than the Debbie Downers. I strive to be a Normal Nancy.

Of course, there are secondary gains for writing: I also like to think of writing, especially blogging, to send little messages through the week to those of you who may be having a rough week …sort of an "I'm still here" nudge to get you back on track. Sometimes the messages are directly aimed toward myself for accountability. For those of you that I have never met, I like to think that my content could push you to find a therapist in your city, to seek out DBT® (as that is my theoretical orientation and if you like me, you will like DBT®) for yourself.

I am not harping on who I am just to toot my own horn; rather, I would like to illustrate the importance of identity! So many of the problems we are going to explore in this book are a direct result of having an unstable identity. What I have found as a therapist, is that the clients who do not get better, don't know who they are! They are not part of any sort of community that helps define their values and morals. Have you heard the adage that "if you don't stand for something, you'll fall for anything"? I am not going to lie, before I knew who I was, I tried on a variety of identities: punky-goth kid, overachieving student, laid-back/go-with-the-flow friend, hippy chick …The greatest part of my experimenting is that it has allowed me to develop a greater understanding for what you are going through. None of us have it truly figured out. The best thing we can do is to make choices along the way that help us feel more competent and self-respecting. I have no idea what "type" I am today, which is AWESOME! I dislike personality inventories and diagnoses; labels belong on soup cans and cereal boxes. I have taken the best parts of my past selves …and molded them into the me that I am today. For once, I can say I am proud of who I am.

I had to work hard and turn down a lot of other opportunities to get to where I am today; this means that I decided ahead of time what my goals were, and I used every skill I knew to achieve my long-term goals. There were jobs along the way that I turned down, despite better pay, because they did not lead down my desired path. There were family events that I missed out on because I was studying or training. There have been concerts, movies, trips, etc. that I chose not to experience if they used too many of my resources in that moment. This does NOT mean that I have not had fun in the past 12 years; I have! I have vacationed to the Caribbean twice (one trip solo!), I have taken road trips across the country, I have lounged by the pool, I have become a parent, I have repainted my house, I have spent too much money on Michael Kors handbags …AND I will tell you that all the healthy decisions I made were made with intention, on purpose, with no regret. That is the Adulting Well difference. Adulting Well using DBT® skills will allow you to be spontaneous and have an enjoyable life, while reaching your goals! Please join me; I want nothing more than to share in your journey and be a stepping stone on the path toward the life you want to lead. Achieving your long-term goals will require you to learn different ways of interacting with your emotions and different ways of communicating your needs to others, all-the-while being honest and working to accept the realities of your life, our world, and any associated limitations!

What:

Dialectical Behavioral Therapy is a unique and holistic mental health treatment that has been researched and found effective to treat nearly every single mental health disorder. It was originally created by Marsha Linehan to treat Borderline Personality Disorder and chronic suicidality; however, in the last 20+ years it has been discovered to be a bit of a miracle cure for all of life's mental ailments (and some physical ones). A 2014 study by Goodman et al. found that post-DBT, people show less reactivity in their amygdala overall! This is amazing news, as your amygdala is the part of your brain that aids in your interpreting and experiencing emotions. Less reactivity means more skillful responding (and likely less regret)! Linehan believes that based on the biosocial theory, people learn to self-harm or develop a propensity for other maladaptive coping attempts such as avoidance of problems and feelings (substance abuse, aggressive venting, overspending, promiscuity, gambling, eating disorders, etc.) to regulate their emotional dysregulation …DBT® shows us that there is another way! Furthermore, for those that might find themselves deep in the pit of despair, DBT® is recommended by the National Registry of Evidence-based Programs and Practices for the psychosocial treatment, co-occurring disorders, and mental health inpatient treatment. It is also the number one evidence-based treatment for suicidality according to the National Institute of Mental Health.

An encouraging bit of news is that a study in 2005 found that people who can effectively regulate their emotions tend towards better physical health (Carre et al, 2005), and another found that people with effective emotion regulation abilities report higher levels of relationship qualities (Levenson et al, 1994). I have certainly experienced both findings to be true in my life and the lives of my clients. Learning to regulate our emotions without quick-fixes or avoidance will open the door and allow us to walk towards the goals we have set for our future selves more efficiently.

As with all therapy and problem solving, DBT® only works if you WORK and put in the TIME. You will be asked to put in mental and physical effort throughout this journey. Change does not happen overnight. If there was a self-help book that had all the answers or a pill that fixed everything, I would tell you and gladly retire! Adulting well will require sustained effort and diligence. I truly feel blessed to teach skills classes each week as it keeps me "on point" with my own adulting and mental health habits! DBT® has been adapted for nearly any sub-specialization you may be suffering from. A quick Amazon.com book search uncovers over 800 different books (at the time of writing), ranging on topics from DBT for parents of intense children to DBT workbooks for bipolar adolescents. There is no book to date; however, to address the unique skills needed to navigate the art of adulting. This book is for everyone over the age of 16; it is not a book only for millennials, 20 somethings, or college students. It is for anyone trying to wrap their heads around how-to adult well. I have found that the same mental hang-ups cause distress for high school students, young adults, college students, parents, empty-nesters, middle aged adults, etc. I believe our culture does not promote healthy behaviors which could free you from the stress and suffering of your day-to-day life. As a culture, we MUST shift from short term, instant gratification, and move toward long-term gains (which can be painful sometimes)! When we make choices mindfully, we can handle the short-term discomfort associated with our urges in order to reach our goals. We learn to have trust in our decision making. There is freedom in learning to tolerate discomfort. The adulting well skills are what you need to achieve this freedom. Consider this simple example:

Do you order the same thing every time you are at certain restaurants? Just because an appetizer or a soda sounds good does not mean you have to order it! Are you able to break behavioral patterns (i.e., I ALWAYS order a Coke) in order to make a mindful choice with less regret (i.e., Today, a Shirley Temple sounds really good!) Are you willing to entertain the waiter's explanation of today's specials, or do you always order the same thing? These skills will show you that you can break free of your patterns and habits.

The skills in these pages will show you:

1. How to make decisions that are aligned with the life you WANT and the values you have.

2. What skills to use to tolerate the (short-term) discomfort associated with sacrificing something you want now, to achieve what you want for your long-term future goals.

3. How to accept the hand you were dealt and stop setting fires to the progress you have made.

4. How to lead a much simpler and much more contented lifestyle, thus reducing new suffering.

Who doesn't want that!?

In this book, you will have the opportunity to participate in this process. At various points, you will be invited to reflect on a prompt via journaling. I urge you to read the chapters slowly, take notes, underline, and really pause at the reflections. I even encourage you to wait a day before (and possibly even after) reading and journaling. You may even find it helpful to journal after each chapter, then wait a week and re-read the chapter. I want this book to be like a meal you savor. Sustained change takes time. We can all commit to change a habit after reading a post on social media, but do we REALLY change? I don't want you to have reader's indigestion ...so go slow, savor each nugget, and allow yourself time to digest.

Reflect: In what areas are you making emotionally based choices?

Consider the following areas. Do you tend to give into short-term impulses in any specific areas?

☐   Food/eating

_____

_____

_____

Ex: *sugar snack when mid-day fatigue sets in*

☐   Time management (working/playing)

_____

_____

_____

Ex: scrolling social media to avoid responsibilities

☐   Anger impulses

_____

_____

_____

Ex: *impulsively texting back*

☐   Social Anxiety

_____

_____

_____

Ex: *late cancelling social plans*

☐   Fears

_____

_____

_____

Ex: *avoiding crowds and attending events even though you want to go*

☐   Sleep schedule

_____

_____

_____

Ex: *staying up later than planned binge-watching a series*

☐   Self-harming behaviors

_____

_____

_____

Ex: *self-harming after making a mistake*

☐ Substance abuse

_____

_____

_____

Ex: *using drugs (illegal or legal) to regulate or avoid emotions*

☐ Emotional urges

_____

_____

_____

Ex: y*elling at someone, eye-rolling, door slamming*

☐ Trying to "fit in"

_____

_____

_____

Ex: *pretending you like something that you really do not just to get approval*

Are you able to identify any areas that you do well in exercising restraint against urges and making more mindful choices?

_____

_____

_____

_____

_____

_____

_____

_____

_____

Where:

I would certainly encourage you to find a local DBT® skills class in your city as a foundation/adjunct to this class. I adamantly support the model and believe (perhaps I would dare to say I guarantee) that attending a DBT® skills class is the most efficient and cost-effective method to learn and master the skills in the shortest amount of time. An adherent and effective skills class meets weekly for one year, going through the skill material twice. They will have you meet with an individual therapist during that time and track your moods/urges/actions on a diary card every day. If you find a program that is not doing that, keep looking! If that type of program is not an option for you, I encourage you to use this book and the DBT Skills Training Handouts and Worksheets by Marsha Linehan (hereafter referred to as the Linehan Skills Training book) to self-study and start changing your life. Also use the internet, which has loads of examples, videos, blogs, websites etc. There is no such thing as having TOO many resources! Aside from entering your city + Dialectical Behavioral Therapy into a web browser, you can go to www.tara4bpd.org or www.behavioraltech.org for a reputable list of DBT® trained therapists.

Please make yourself a sanctuary space. It is important that you choose a DIFFERENT place in your home than where you kick back to watch TV or eat dinner. If you sit in those spaces, you will quickly revert to those behaviors due to your own habituation. For example: in my home, sitting on the far-left couch cushion (my chillin' spot is the far-right cushion) and making a mug of hot tea, is my cue that mental health optimization is about to occur. I have a lamp on the left side of the couch with a BRIGHT LED light bulb in it, I tend to light a candle, use my favorite pens that I reserve only for journaling, get comfy with a blanket and pillows, and turn my phone on silent. If I sit on the far-right cushion (my spot), my habituation quickly pulls me into mindless snacking and watching television. The left side cushion pattern has really become a habit that tells my brain and body that real mental work is about to occur. I urge you to be fired-up and PASSIONATE about this. Your mental well-being is at stake!

I will do my best to explain all skills I am referring to; however, please note that I am not teaching you all the skills! You can use the Linehan

Skills Training book to access the DBT® skillset in its entirety. This book will become nothing more than a fancy decoration on your bookshelf if you do not use it in the way it was intended. Part of my humanness is that I, too, have an affinity for purchasing self-help books and workbooks. I, too, fall into reading and not practicing or only reading the first three chapters! I intend to get to the worksheets or journaling soon …later …when I feel like it. I URGE you not to skip the workbook pages or journaling. I know that would be my first urge; I always want to know the ending to a story before I begin reading. The results come from doing the hard work. An overarching theme you will discover in this book is the requirement for you to tolerate doing things in the short term that may be unpleasant SO THAT you can reach your long-term goals. Once again, you will need to use the skills I teach to cope with your urges to skip the workbook pages or skip the journaling. You may find yourself wanting to read it first and practice the skills later, please heed this warning and tolerate your distress! It would benefit you so much more to read and practice one chapter at time. There is no suggested time frame for how long one chapter, or one skill should take you; rather, I encourage you to practice each idea presented in a variety of settings, with a variety of emotions and at a variety of intensities. Keep practicing until you feel a sense of competency over the skill. And when you finish the book, re-read it one additional time. What I have found with skills class is that the first time through the material, I am trying to convince clients to "trust me." I (and veteran group members) say things like:

"This will get clearer as time goes on."

"I am cross-referencing a skill that you haven't learned yet; please be patient."

"It gets easier!"

As time goes on in DBT® I hear clients say things like:

"I get it now!"

"It's like someone turned on all the lights and I can see how all of the skills can work together."

"I finally see the picture you've been talking about!"

Research on DBT® also shows that when people go through the material one time and then drop out of skills class, they quickly regress right back to where they started. I have seen this play out many times and it is heartbreaking because if you do the work, you ought to reap the benefits! Once again …do the hard work! Read the book once slowly and then once a bit quicker. You deserve to fully get the material. You deserve to live your best life.

When:

I suggest that you create a bit of a ritual when working on this book.

Just as if you are/were attending a skills class, which would be held at the same time/day each week, at the same location with perhaps a treat of a latte before or after …create that sort of structure for yourself with this book. Sometimes I fight against it (wahhh wahhh wahhh, I want to binge-watch a pointless show or mindlessly eat chips), yet EVERY single time I engage in my home-therapy behavior, my sense of self improves. My shame of binge-watching or chip-eating is averted. My sense of pride and accomplishment grows. Humor me and give it a try! I want you to have the sense of accomplishment and pride that you have been missing out on for far too long. You deserve to feel a sense of pride around your mature adulting behavior!

Why: This one is up to you.

- ☐ Are you sick and tired of being sick and tired?
- ☐ Are you tired of your reputation (at work, within your family, etc.)?
- ☐ Are you ready to stop living paycheck-to-paycheck?
- ☐ Are you eager to learn how to make peace with doing things alone (i.e., shopping, movies, lunch)?
- ☐ Are you tired of letting your emotions decide what you do from hour to hour?
- ☐ Are you ready to stop letting how many followers, friends, etc. that you have define how you feel about yourself?
- ☐ Are you ready for a life that leaves you feeling a sense of pride?
- ☐ Are you ready to be the one that your friends look to for advice, instead of the person they go to for venting only?
- ☐ Are you ready to stop living with that sense of regret, shame, guilt, and/or loneliness?

If you answered yes to ANY of those questions, it sounds like it is time to make a change. I can help.

Let's do this.

Pre-Test: Self-Assessment - Who are you now?

Before you begin the work presented in this book, let's take a snapshot of who you are currently.

Name: _____

Age: _____

Occupation: _____

How would you rate your ability to tolerate urges in the areas mentioned below, on a scale of 0-5 (0= no control, 3 = moderate control and 5 = complete control)?

- Financial urges: _____
- Time management urges: _____
- Anger urges: _____
- Anxiety urges: _____
- Substance abuse urges: _____
- Self-harm urges: _____
- Peer-pressure urges: _____
- Sad urges: _____
- Food related urges: _____

I believe my biggest strengths are:

I believe I need to grow/change in the following areas:

I am satisfied with these areas of my life:

I am dissatisfied with these areas of my life:

2 WHAT IS DBT® AND WHY SHOULD I CARE?

In short, Dialectical Behavioral Therapy is a type of mental health therapy that pulls from both behavioral and cognitive strategies to really maximize the change you will see in your life. DBT® takes a non-blaming approach and utilizes biosocial theory to explain how you got to where you are and why you act the way you do. Biosocial theory explains that we are all a combination of our biology (genes, hereditary conditions, etc.) and our social environment factors (averse experiences, cultural differences, childhood, family dynamics). Biosocial theory proposes that the cause of a person having problems with emotional and behavioral control is the result of the hand we were dealt, so to speak. Take for instance a person who has a solid biological set up: mentally healthy parents, no sensory issues, a general "tough cookie," and place them into a life of adversity: poverty, loss of parent(s), childhood sexual abuse, transient housing, etc. That person is likely to develop behavioral and emotional patterns that are less than stellar (mostly due to the social environment). Another person could be genetically screwed (so to speak): hitting every biological risk factor as they fall through the family tree. They could have attended a great school, had a wholesome friend group and a loving family, had no traumatic experiences …and they could come out with the same set of problem behaviors as the first person. In reality, we are all usually somewhere in the middle. We have a few genetic risk factors and a few adverse experiences early in life. As I said, this is a non-blaming approach. You do not get to blame your mother and refuse to change. You do not get to blame your genetics and wither away. Having this knowledge provides us with insight and allows us room to grow and evolve!

This chapter might seem dense and overwhelming; however, a foundation must be built for future understanding to be built upon.

What are some of your biological risk factors?

- ☐ Family history
- ☐ Chronic, progressive, or terminal diagnosis
- ☐ Female
- ☐ Over age 65
- ☐ LGBTQAI+
- ☐ Addiction
- ☐ Going through hormonal changes (puberty/menopause)

- ☐ Other: _____

And what are your social risk factors?

- ☐ Single, widowed, divorced.
- ☐ Victim of physical, emotional and/or sexual abuse
- ☐ History of being bullied.
- ☐ Under-employed
- ☐ Financial trouble
- ☐ Inability to focus.
- ☐ Isolated
- ☐ Job dissatisfaction
- ☐ Recent loss or life change

- ☐ Other: _____

Take a moment to reflect in your journal as to how this combination of factors has led to your current mental functioning, for the better or worse. Can you do this, without blame or judgment? (If not, it is ok …I will teach you how!)

The next major thing to understand is what the heck dialectical behavioral therapy is! I sincerely hope they never delete the video. Assuming it is still live, please go to YouTube and check out What is Dialectical Behavioral Therapy for Adolescents by UC San Francisco. They do a fantastic job of laying it out! For this book, let's unpack one thing at a time:

Skill: Dialectics (I will always introduce a skill in this way)

The first idea to understand is what "dialectical" means. Dialectical refers to the concept that two ideas that oppose one another can both contain truth! This is EARTHSHATTERING once your wrap your head around it. The skill of "calling the dialectic" allows us to work toward establishing and validating the truth on both sides, rather than fighting to disprove one side or the other. You will see that clinging to "your" side will only produce and increase suffering. You will have to stop playing tug-of-war with oak trees (i.e., your stubborn loved ones, when you are just as stubborn)! What I often see in families/marriages is frequent fights and bickering over nothing of significance which leads to fights of great significance.

For example:
Me: *"Where do you want to go to dinner?"*
Them: *"Um …how about Italian? Eggplant parmesan sounds SO GOOD!"*
Me: *"Ugh …no …I want a burger."* (not validating at all, just giving examples)
Them: *"Well then why did you even ask me?"* (reacting due to perceived threat)
Me: *"What's your problem? I was just talking out loud. Whatever …fine …we can get Italian."*
Them: *"Forget it. I'm staying home."*

Sound familiar? What we teach in DBT® is how to see the commonalities and work WITH the other person, rather than against them. We must learn to validate (more on this later in this chapter) any and all parts of the other person's point of view. This will immediately reduce their emotional reaction! Validation means that you find something about the other person's experience that is valid (makes sense) to you or would likely make sense to someone in their experience and reflect it to them out loud. That is it, validate and stop. Our natural urge is to partially validate and then either "one up" the other person or try to give them advice on how to fix their problem. This damages relationships though; unless someone WANTS your opinion or feedback, do not give it. In the above example, both people are hungry. Both people are both motivated to go out to a restaurant. Instead of perceiving an argument/threat, I will show you below how to validate and join with the other person. Let's start there …

Me: *"Where do you want to go to dinner?"*
Them: *"Oooh …good idea! I AM hungry!"* (validating the idea)
Me: *"Me too …I was thinking we should go out somewhere for comfort food, you?"*
Them: *"I can get behind that idea! I am tired and don't want to do dishes. Are you up for Italian, American, Mexican …?"* (validating what makes sense about going out to eat)

Me: "I hear ya, we have had a long week! For some reason …a burger sounds good to me. Would you be ok with that?"

Them: "For sure, I am not craving anything specific …I am sure I can find something good on the menu; let's go!"

Look at the difference there. Just by joining with and validating the other person, the conversation goes so much smoother. We encourage mindful communication in DBT®, which means engaging non-judgmentally and curiously into the conversation, slowing down so that both people are heard, and really participating in the conversation –rather than clinging to one side so rigidly.

Dialectics can be applied in all arenas of your life; I promise we will get a lot of practice at figuring out how to do this effectively! In order to be dialectical, I strongly encourage you to work on being curious. Having curiosity about another person's opinions can be a great tool as you will be naturally less judgmental and more open to seeing why they have that view. Dialectical thinking will make people flock to you because it permits you to be a more easygoing friend; everyone wants to talk to/spend time with someone who is open to new ideas!

Dialectical dilemmas are when we are in the tug-of-war. They can also happen internally. I will admit, these can get a bit tricky. An internal dialectical dilemma is when you are at war with yourself, ceaselessly arguing with yourself. These dilemmas are exhausting and make you less fun to be around as you will be a bit on edge. As an anxious person myself, I often get into dialectical arguments with myself over whether to attend a social event or whether to stay home.

When you find yourself in these battles, internally or externally, the trick is to notice it and work on finding the synthesis (a fusion of the two sides that validates at least one thing on each side). See the example on the next page.

Skill: Dialectics

A dialectical dilemma is when you are experiencing the impasse associated with clinging to your strongly held belief, while blocking any understanding of the other person's point of view. These can also happen internally, when you are arguing with yourself over the best course of action. I will show you two examples:

The first example is a common internal dilemma that happens for people, usually resulting in anxiety. In the boxes on each side of the dialectical diagram (aka the "teeter totter"), you will see the opposing thoughts. Think of these as the thoughts at war with one another. Under each box, you see statements as to why the thought is valid (makes sense). The large center box are ideas that are a "win-win," in that at least one thing from each side is met.

I don't want to go to the family function.

I need to go to the family function.

It is the last day of nice weather this week.

Cousin Jane will be there, she annoys me.

Everyone will ask if I am dating anyone.

I won't be able to run my errands today.

I have had a long week at work.

I am tired.

Obligation

My mom will hound me if I don't go.

I can brag about my promotion.

If I am there, they can't talk about me.

It might be fun.

Free food/Cake

Possible syntheses:

I can skip it if I take advantage of weather and hike.

I can attend and bring a friend as a buffer.

I can attend yet let them know I have to leave early because I have plans.

I can stay home and schedule lunch with mom tomorrow.

Step one: Identify and fill in the opposing thoughts. This can take some practice; be patient with yourself!

Step two: Drop the stubbornness and curiously explore each side. This means you must breathe and stop clinging to the side that you feel more passionately about RIGHT NOW. This requires you to have compassion with yourself and your thoughts.

Step three: Begin a list under each thought of what makes sense about that point of view. You must come up with answers under each thought, even if they seem silly or you have judgments about writing them down. You may need to ask others for help here or take breaks and come back to it. Questions to ask yourself are:

    1. Why is this thought/point of view valid?

    2. What do I want to achieve if I take this position?

Step four: Work on coming up with syntheses. These are win-win ideas in which you meet at least one goal from the list on each side. It will not always be 50/50; however, you will feel less frustration and more peace with the decision as you have figured out a way to honor BOTH sides!

Dialectical dilemmas also occur between yourself and other people. Sometimes this is you vs a peer, sometimes it is you vs an organizational rule, sometimes it is you vs your family. Dialectical dilemmas that include another person include at least twice the emotion! Let's take a look at this idea:

My spouse wants to take vacation with our kids, driving 16 hours to Disney World.	I want to take several small "stay-cations" within 2 hours driving distance.
We would be making great memories.	Smaller blocks of time in car make kids happier.
The kids love Disney movies.	Spread money spent out over months.
It would give us a LOT of time to talk.	Allow kids to experience variety of things.
We used to enjoy road trips.	Family time
We can afford it right now	Fun for everyone

Possible syntheses:

We could do 5 days in Disney with several stops on the way.

We could let kids help choose.

Step one: The first step is to identify and fill in the opposing thoughts. This can take some practice, remove all judgments, and stick to the facts. "My husband is an idiot" is not the correct thought to fill in!

Step two: Drop the stubbornness and curiously explore each side. Remember: YOU are not right. You BOTH are right. This means you must breathe and stop clinging to the side that you feel more passionately about. This requires you to have compassion with yourself and your spouse, your ideas, AND his ideas! Fill out the validating statements as if the other side does not exist. This reduces getting right back into tug of war. IE: do not write "Staycation is less time in car than 16-hour drive to Disney"

Step three: Begin a list under each thought of what makes sense about that point of view. You must come up with answers under each thought, even if they seem silly or you have judgments about writing them down. If you block your thoughts, they will only fester. You may need to ask others for help here or take breaks and come back to it. Questions to ask yourself are:

1. Why is this thought/point of view valid?

2. What do I want to achieve if I take this position? (even if it is not YOUR idea, what could you get out of choosing that point of view?)

Step four: Work on coming up with syntheses. These are win-win ideas in which you meet at least one goal from the list on each side. It won't always be 50/50; however, you will feel less frustration and more peace with the decision as you honored BOTH sides!

You can draw blank diagrams for your additional practice!

Example/common dilemmas that arise internally are:

- I want to quit my job vs I need stable income.
- I want to show good work ethic vs the urge to slack off/relax.
- I want to stay in bed today vs responsibilities at home or office.
- I want to love my body vs I want to lose weight.
- I want to go buy _____ vs I am saving for _____
- I want to _____ vs a group that you belong to wants to _____
- I want to eat healthy vs the ease of eating conveniently.
- Relax vs run errands.
- Share on social media vs keep private.

Example/Common dilemmas that arise within relationships/eternally are:

- The family wants pizza every night vs I believe we should eat healthy meals.

- My teen wants a later curfew for an event vs I should stick to my guns.
- My team likes to meet on Tuesday mornings vs I want to move the meeting to Fridays.
- My spouse likes dinner cooked nightly vs I like to cook on weekends for the whole week.
- Follow dress code vs individuality.
- Tell on/Report something to authorities' vs keeps information secret
- Prioritize "me time" vs Prioritize family/group demands.

You know you are in a dialectical dilemma when you are passionately clinging to your point of view and experiencing a lot of emotions about someone trying to "change your mind." In general, we all need to learn how to cooperate and work together. It may be inconvenient for you to not get your way; however, very rarely is it as much of a catastrophe as you think it will be. Being dialectical is going to require you to approach situations differently and choose to respond in a way that may feel unfamiliar. It might be hard to admit; however, you, nor I, are always right! It does get easier with practice …you MUST practice and practice often if you want things to improve.

Behaviorism

The second idea we need to explore to understand is to understand Dialectical Behavioral Therapy is the behavioral part. "Behavioral" alludes to the fact that I am going to ask you to change (some of) your behaviors (actions). The idea here is that you (at times) are MAKING IT WORSE for yourself! Your actions/behaviors/choices are leading to INCREASED suffering! Once we realize this, we can open the door to new ideas, be experimental with trying new ways of acting, and start making choices that support the life you want to live, rather than hinder any progress. Think back to the restaurant example given in chapter one. Have you fallen into a pattern of "always" ordering chicken tenders because you are afraid of trying new foods? Is this making you suffer because you experience envy when you see/sample what other people have ordered? Do you experience shame when people tease you about your habits? This can be generalized to many areas: how we drive, how we clean, etc.

Behaviorism is a concept that can literally encompass an entire college degree; however, there are some components that I would like you to understand:

1. reinforcement: a reinforcer is anything that increases the likelihood that a behavior will occur again. Reinforcers can be positive (as in something ADDED) or negative (as in something SUBTRACTED) and either type achieve the same goal of increasing the odds that a behavior will continue. Examples of positive reinforcers include verbal praise, eye contact, hugs, rewards programs at stores, stickers, or a paycheck. Negative reinforcers can be a bit more difficult to wrap our heads around. Most often, people assume a negative reinforcer is a punishment, which is incorrect. Examples of negative reinforcers include: Chap Stick (as it removes chapped lips, thus reinforcing the likelihood that you will use it again), the dinging of your seatbelt (as it will end when you buckle up) and nagging (as the nagging will end -be subtracted- when you do the desired behavior). These are usually things that we want and will work to earn, whether they are positive or negative reinforcers.

2. Punishment: punishment is the addition of an aversive in an effort to get the person to stop engaging in a behavior. Punishments are the LEAST effective way to get someone to change and are the most common method we resort to. Punishments do not teach the person what else to do and are often unrelated to the offense or are nonsensical. Think about it in real life: When the bank charges you a fee for over-drafting …does that make you not overdraft in the future or does it just frustrate and shame you? In reality, you would not have over-drafted on purpose, so it doesn't really make sense! It makes you want to AVOID the bank and checking your balance (I wonder if this is why they do it? Not checking is a result of your anxiety and actually helps them make MORE money!). When a person is locked up for failure to pay child support, that person is not taught another way to make money and also tends to lose their job as a result! This one is counterproductive and ineffective. Screaming at teenagers and taking their phone for misbehavior does not actually do anything to improve their motivation for new behavior; rather, it tends to increase the likelihood that they will lie and hide their behaviors from you while also building resentment.

3. Consequence – A consequence is anything that happens naturally in response to a behavior. They can be positive or negative. A consequence of exercise is a more toned body and more energy. A consequence of studying is better grades. Both are positive natural consequences that reinforce the behaviors. If people avoid you due to foul body odor or if you break down after ignoring your gas gauge light, you are experiencing natural negative consequences. These are preferred to punishments. Natural consequences do encompass the idea of letting kids fail sometimes or letting yourself get into "trouble" occasionally, to promote learning. Consider the idea of teaching a man to fish vs giving a man a fish.

4. Extinction burst – this is a phenomenon that happens when you are giving up a behavior (addiction) and all of a sudden it re-surfaces with a vengeance! In general, if you ignore it (i.e., do not reinforce it by paying it a lot of attention) it will go away. I see it as an effort for your brain to try "one more time" before really admitting that it is not something you want to keep doing.

Reflect by Journaling:
- What are you doing that IS NOT helping you reach your goals? (Be specific; these are your BEHAVIORS that we need to work on decreasing) Examples may include not following through with tasks, self-harm, substance abuse, arguing with people, being late.
- Why do you engage in behaviors that you know are not helpful? What is reinforcing the behaviors? Examples may include people coming to help you, relief from stress, the illusion of being in charge …
- What thought patterns do you notice that get in your way? Examples may include that you turn to these behaviors when anxious to seek a sense of control or you learned these behaviors from your parents and you only resort back to them in their presence.
- What do you do when you are experiencing discomfort (physical pain, disagreements with others, financial urges)? Is that a helpful or a harmful pattern?
- What behaviors do you want to do more of?
- What thought patterns would you like to nurture and grow?
- How would you like people to describe you?
- Who do you want to emulate? Do you have a role model who seems to cope well with life's ups and downs?

Take some time to journal on these questions as they may prompt you to dive a bit deeper into these topics.

Acceptance Vs Change

DBT® makes a big deal out of acceptance AND change. Hmm …can you spot the dialectic here? Accepting a problem and working to change a situation are in complete contrast with one another! And yet they are both necessary and contain truths to unlock the life you want to live! Let's plug them into the dialectical diagram:

Acceptance	Change
Allows us to ride the waves of life with less distress.	Recognizes that we do have choices.
Honors the fact that some things are out of our hands.	Empowers us to problem solve.
Permits us to relax.	Decreases likelihood of repeat crises.
Mindful living decreases negative emotions and increases a sense of connection and validity.	We become less dependent on others.
	We are no longer slaves to our emotions.

Syntheses:

DBT has a both-and philosophy. We learn what we can change, what we need to accept, and how to differentiate between the two.

If you only ever worked on acceptance, you'd become a bit of a doormat. If you currently are a doormat …we need to look at what parts of life ought to be accepted and which parts ought to be changed. Newsflash: not EVERTHING falls into acceptance! Let's grow a backbone and push back a bit! A short list of things to accept:

- Your diagnoses
- The diagnoses of your loved ones
- Your family's personalities
- Your CURRENT take home pay
- Your CURRENT living situation
- Who your family is.
- Deaths of loved ones
- War/Terrorism/Criminal behaviors
- Your past choices

If you only ever worked on change, you would be a bit neurotic. I prefer to use the phrase "type A," but it's semantics really. Pushing for change non-stop is EXHAUSTING and you will drive yourself crazy! Sorry to be the bearer of bad news …there are things in life outside of your control (see the list above)! A short list of things we can work to change:

- Your outlook on situations
- What you say/do
- Who you allow into your presence.
- Whether you follow medical advice/diets/exercise
- Where you are employed and/or living
- Your patterns and thus your future choices

DBT® seeks to teach the acceptance and change skills via the four core modules. These are explained in depth in the Skills Training Handouts and Worksheets book by Marsha Linehan. The change skills are taught in the emotion regulation module and the interpersonal effectiveness module. The key idea here is that if we work to change how YOU communicate with the world and what YOU do when you start to feel things, the consequence is that YOUR life experience will improve. Note: YOU cannot change how other people communicate or what they do when they start to feel things! The acceptance skills are taught in the mindfulness module and in the distress tolerance module. The key idea here is that YOU must become more aware and wake up to your automatic tendencies, and YOU have to start to realize when you are in a crisis, and YOU have to stop making it worse. Note: You do not have to accept being treated poorly; rather, you need to open your eyes to when it is happening and then use the change skills to change the situation. You need to be willing to feel your feelings. I promise that if you run from them, ignore them, or stuff them down the consequence is that they WILL keep bubbling up to the surface, with more and more force each time. Second note: this is not meant to be blaming. It is a core assumption in DBT® that while you did not cause all your life's problems, you must learn to heal from them. I make the analogy that if you had friends over for a Super Bowl party and they made a mess (then they went home) you might feel frustrated about the clean-up, as you did not make the mess. The reality is that if you want to have a clean home again, YOU must clean it up (or hire someone to clean it up). You hold the power to reduce your own suffering. It will take a mindset shift and a hefty dose of acceptance; however, I will lead the way.

Recognizing acceptance and change

What are some components of how you communicate that could use some change?

Ex: I would like to learn to walk away and calm myself before reacting in anger

What are some things you would like to change regarding how you handle emotions? Are there specific emotions that you struggle with more?

Ex: I would like to learn to cope more effectively with sadness, instead of staying in bed

In what areas would you like to be more accepting?

> *Ex: I would love to learn how to accept the daily things that are not in my control, like traffic and other people's behaviors*

In what relationships do you need to work to stop trying to change the other person?

> *Ex: I need to stop trying to change my brother; it is ruining our relationship*

In what ways do you need to accept life being out of control (at times) so that you stop making it worse?

> *Ex: When I feel rejected, I would like to stop resorting to self-harm*

Do you notice that there are certain relationships that you struggle with?

> *Ex: I struggle with my co-worker Pete. I feel a sense of competition with him, which makes me reactive and I likely look foolish to our boss.*

Are their certain people that seem to be able to get you so worked up that you engage in power struggles, thus making it worse?

Are you willing to work on yourself? _____
Are you willing to stop blaming others? _____
Are you willing to admit that you cannot change other people? _____

Spoiler alert: We will uncover a "yes" for each of those three questions before you finish this book.

If any of the above questions prompted strong feelings, stop here and journal more on that topic.

Validation

How much different would your life be if people told you that your perceptions were appropriate? How amazing would it feel if someone noticed how hard you work? The last underlying topic that you need to understand before stepping into this book is the idea of validation and its close relative self-validation. Validation is a skill that our culture truly struggles with. To validate someone requires you to be able to step into their shoes for a moment and find something about their perspective or experience that makes sense (we call this the kernel of truth). A 2011 study by Shenk and Fruzetti found that people that interact in an invalidating environment (home, school, work, society) regularly had significantly higher levels of negative affect/emotions and elevated heart rate when compared to those in a validating environment. Overtime this leads to poorer physical health as the above issues will cause undue wear and tear on your body. Invalidating environments increase emotional reactivity during times of stress (even among people who typically handle stress well!). Validation in an environment leads to a steady decline in heart rate and no change in affect (the ability to stay more emotionally level). Validation is powerful for us physically and emotionally!

On the days where you are so depressed and the literal best you can do is to get out of bed and wear pajamas, what would it mean for you to hear a validating statement such as, "Given your depression and the recent rainy week, I understand why you would want to stay in comfortable clothes; depression makes it seem pointless to get dressed?" On the days that you are so anxious that you end up being late to work due the need to cheer lead yourself out of the house or the intensity of your IBS (irritable bowel syndrome) symptoms, what would it mean for you to hear a validating statement such as, "I have a hard time going to family functions when I know it will be crowded. I wonder if it is a similar feeling to the anxiety you are feeling today?" When you are working on giving up a behavior that no one in your family understands, what would it mean if someone said, "I can understand why you would turn to _____ as a way to cope with your stress." It would be such a different world if people took time to TRY and understand why other humans do what we do instead of jumping straight toward judgment.

To validate is not to agree. Re-read the italicized sentences in the previous paragraph. I am not saying "you should stay in pajamas" or "staying home is the right thing to do" or "just keep self-harming if it works so well"! Fear of the other person perceiving agreement is the biggest complaint I hear about this skill. Please note, you can validate a person's emotions without validating their actions. If someone punches a hole in the wall you could say, "I can see that you are really frustrated by this" without saying, "I can see that you are really frustrated by this, and I would totally punch a hole in the drywall, too!" You can validate a person's emotion, their urge, their action, their beliefs, or just the facts of the situation. We validate what is valid. Eisenberg & Fabes (1994) and Shipman et al. (2000) found that teens are more effective in regulating their own emotions when their parents respond with validation (warmth and attention) and a 2002 study from Gottman & Levenson found that couples who are more validating are more likely to remain married! The good news on validation as a skill is that no matter who you are validating, the relationship is likely to improve if you use it!

There are levels of intensity with validation to consider; we select our level based on how authentically we can be in the given situation.

In choosing a level of validation, be authentic! The other person will be able to tell if you are fake and it will sound like you are mocking them, which is more invalidating than just ignoring them! Higher level is not always more effective. Can you imagine how a therapy session would go if your therapist always cried when you cried, laughed when you laughed, etc. … We need to focus more on which level is more effective, given the relationship and the situation.

Self-validation is turning the skill inward instead of trying to talk yourself out of your experience. Have you ever experienced an injustice and then tried to convince yourself that it wasn't that bad? Self-validation is to say, "that did hurt my feelings" or "I am tearful today and that is ok" or "I think other people would be annoyed by that, too!"

Validation in both forms is essential for emotion regulation. When we perceive that we are wrong or that others are judging our experience, we tend to become more emotional. A simple validation from another person and/or self-validating statement can soothe the inflamed emotion and help you return to a more stable state of mind, thus improving your ability to problem solve.

I truly hope that this book will be a validating offering to you. There is no way that you would know how to adult well if you weren't taught it! I can speak from my knowledge base that for the most part, our culture does not teach emotional regulation or problem solving. Just turn on the television to see that our world reinforces ineffective behaviors! Teenage parents are given TV shows, people utilizing public benefits are cut off immediately if they start making money, and "freaking out" is often the fastest way to get family and friend support. I hope to offer you ways to get your needs met that also leave you walking away from the experience with your self-respect.

Low level validation

High level validation

- Give eye contact, lean in, nod.

- Reflect back what you are hearing:
  "you are angry about _____, is that correct?"

- Read between the lines:
  "it sounds like a lot has piled up today."
  Be curious:
  "you say you are fine, yet your body language looks sad."

- Express to them understanding of their point of view and how it makes sense:
  "Given the experience you have had with that company, I can see why you'd be angry."

- Express how you/most people would also feel that way in their circumstances.
  "I think if I received that letter in the mail, I'd be scared, too!"

- Feel the feeling with them (i.e., celebrations, funerals, good news, bad news"

Skill Practice: Validation
Jot down some examples below of successes you have had recently!

Successes in self-validation:
Example: *It made sense that I cried today; getting unexpected bad news is difficult.*

Successes in validation of others:
Example: *I can see why my boss reprimanded my team today; we didn't finish the project by the agreed upon deadline.*

Examples of when I have felt validated:
Example: *When my friend sent a celebration GIF in response to me telling her I found the shoes I'd been looking for.*

Examples of when I have felt invalidated:
Example: *When my friend texted "k." when I said I wanted to hang out.*

Examples of when I could have validated myself or others and chose not to:

Example: *I told myself to "get over it" about my friend's text when I know most people find "k." to be hurtful or confusing*

Reflect by journaling:

Who have you experienced as invalidating?
Can you work on validating them?
What is your internal dialogue like? Are you patient and understanding of yourself, or are you self-critical and self-judgmental?
What would life be like if you felt heard and understood?
What would be different if you stopped judging yourself?
Spend some time in your journal on these topics.

3 ADULTING AND WHY IT MATTERS

Learning to adult is not just for young adults. I believe that there is a skillset needed to adult well that is simply not and has not been taught to people in our culture. We are not teaching young people to comprehend and cope with emotional distress and discomfort, which leads to an ever-growing skill deficit. In fact, what I see is that we are teaching each generation of people to avoid discomfort and seek a quick fix whenever possible.

Adult (Noun)
1. One who is fully grown or developed (thanks, Miriam Webster Dictionary!)

My definition of adulting:
Adulting
Verb
1. The practice of behaving in a way characteristic of a responsible adult, especially the accomplishment of mundane but necessary tasks (Oxford dictionary)
2. Getting shit done, even when you don't want to (Alyx's "real life" dictionary)
3. Demonstrating a willingness to follow through on tasks that you don't want to, if they help you reach your long-term goals (i.e., returning calls, doing laundry, paying bills, eating healthily) (Alyx's DBT® translated definition)

It has become evident to me that most people do not know how to do the hard work associated with reaching their goals (because they have not been taught). We live in a world of instant gratification. Most people have not learned the distress tolerance skills needed to persevere along the path to their long-term goals and this distress often leads to self-sabotaging behaviors. This has led to a bit of a boomerang generation, young adults moving back home after trying to live on their own. It is not entirely their fault …how are they supposed to know how to adult when no one taught them? We are an impatient society, and we want instant gratification. We want the quick fix and as soon as our symptoms of distress are alleviated, we regress right back to what we were previously doing…despite evidence to the contrary, despite knowing what got us in over our head in the first place. Adulting will require you to build up a bit of a callus to the pains of life. When we find things to be difficult and they "rub us the wrong way" it is like we get an emotional blister. Adulting requires us to keep at it even when it is difficult, to build up the necessary emotional calluses!

Take some examples:

How many of you take your antibiotic prescription AS PRESCRIBED for the entirety of the recommended prescription? Or run to the doctor for antibiotics without trying to tolerate the symptoms at home? In my experience, most people quit taking their antibiotics about 75% of the way through the recommended course. A large percentage of these people also get mad when their symptoms return (with vengeance) and they need another doctor appointment and stronger medications the second time around. People also have a quick fix mentality and insist on having antibiotics immediately, when the medical field is showing that is not generally recommended. These issues add to the antibiotic resistance we are seeing in the medical field (Shallcross and Davies, 2014).

How many of you like commercial breaks? I remember when commercials would come on network TV during childhood (before DVR!!!) and it was NO.BIG.DEAL. Yet now …how infuriating are the 30 second ads on YouTube! Do you struggle to wait 5 seconds before you can "skip" the ad? Our society can't handle having to wait. Fun fact: a study from 2010 by Nielson found that 45% of DVR recorded commercials are still watched.

How many of you would say you were a good driver when you started out? Always vowing to fill the car with gas when it hit ¼ of a tank, always wearing your seatbelt, never texting when driving, always abiding by the speed limit? And on how many of those things have you slid back from? According to the Center for Disease Control, the number of deaths from distracted driving has been steadily increasing, up to over 3,400 in 2015.

How many of us have a "bedtime," a "diet plan," a "workout routine," …and how many of us keep them? The amount Americans spend on dieting each year continues to rise, up to $65 Billion in 2010 and 90-95% of "dieters" regain all their weight (Bacon & Aphramor, 2011)

As a culture, we have grown lazy and entitled! We want all the results without the hard work! We want what we want, when we want it! Part of real therapy (the kind where you truly get better) is a willingness to do the hard work and a willingness to hear the hard stuff from your therapist without heading for the door. There is also a requirement that you be willing to stick with it. Change does not happen overnight. I am asking you, begging you rather, to do some self-exploration on this topic. The changes I propose in this book will be slow and incremental, this can be hard to face as we seem to want the instant change or the quick fix. Just like to tortoise and the hare, we need to be slow and steady to win this race.

Reflect by journaling: Are you willing to delay gratification and learn to tolerate being uncomfortable for the betterment of your future?

Now that we understand what adulting is and that it will take hard work, we must explore the associated tasks. What tasks are essential to adulting well? I propose that to fully adult; one must be willing to do hard work in the following areas:
• Finances (paying bills, making a budget, understanding investments and retirement)
• Time management (scheduling, tackling task lists, being on time, having down time)
• Employment (finding a job that fits your values, keeping your job, being a good employee)
• Education (finishing or continuing your education, taking adult education courses)
• Personal health and hygiene (making and attending medical appointments, following recommendations, caring for your personal hygiene)
• Physical health (exercise and eating well)
• Social skills (making small talk, attending events as expected, keeping in touch with family and friends)

Furthermore, to set goals in the above areas and reach your goals, you must understand your values! So many of us are not fully aware of what our morals and values are, which causes us to be labile and indecisive. This can manifest itself in falling for peer pressure, acting differently around different groups of people, not standing up for what you believe in (because you aren't sure if you believe it). Remember: if you don't stand for something, you'll fall for anything? Let's be standers, not fallers.

In DBT® your overarching goal set is defined as your "life worth living". DBT® is different because we don't spend all of our time fixating on what ISN'T working; rather, we choose to spend time building the life you want, your life worth living. Once you begin to see growth in those areas, you will spend less and less time ruminating on what ISN'T working and conversely, you will spend more and more time enjoying what IS working for you! The areas listed above are all components of your life worth living.

Skill: Values Assessment

Read through the values list below and circle or highlight the values/qualities that really stand out to you as desirable parts of the life you want. If you don't know what they mean, please look it up as these are not all common terms. Also, feel free to research other lists of values as there are a plethora of lists out there and you may find some values that I did not include!

- Achievement
- Adventure
- Altruism
- Authority
- Balance
- Beauty
- Belonging
- Boldness
- Compassion
- Challenge
- Community
- Contribution
- Creativity
- Curiosity
- Determination
- Enjoyment
- Excitement
- Fairness
- Faith
- Happiness
- Honesty
- Humor
- Independence
- Influence
- Inner Harmony
- Integrity
- Justice

- Kindness
- Knowledge
- Leading by Example
- Learning
- Love
- Loyalty
- Meaningful Work
- Optimism
- Peace
- Personal Growth
- Pleasure
- Popularity
- Recognition
- Reputation
- Respect
- Responsibility
- Security
- Self-Respect
- Service Work
- Spirituality
- Stability
- Success
- Status
- Trustworthiness
- Wealth
- Wisdom

In DBT® we learn that we can take our top values and break them down into goals, then action steps ...thus increasing the odds that you are able to make choices that support your values. When you do this, your self-esteem and self-worth INCREASE (a reinforcer), thus decreasing the likelihood that you will turn to behaviors that are in contrast with your long-term goals. That last line is a loaded statement. I theorize that most of us strive to feel good about who we are and the choices we make. Low self-esteem comes from consistently doing things that do not support our values, and that is often simply because no one has ever taught us to ponder our values and act accordingly. Our culture very much encourages the opposite: instant gratification, do what feels good whenever the heck you want to!

Skill Practice: Values

What are your top three values?

_____

Now pick ONE to prioritize today:

_____

Why is this the one you chose?

_____

_____

_____

_____

What is a measurable goal related to your value?

_____

_____

_____

_____

_____

Examples:
• With the value of competence, the goal may be to read one book per month (or listen to one podcast per week) on a topic that you want to be competent in
• With the value of adventure, the goal may be to explore all the National Parks in America over the next 10 years.
• With the goal of optimism, the goal may be to begin a gratitude journal.

My goal is/My goals are:

_____

_____

_____

_____

_____

We are not done. This is as far as most people get on their own but think about it …the goals are still so big and might feel unattainable. This leads to INACTION which can make us feel worse (a punisher!) and leads to an increased risk of engaging in target behaviors (in DBT® we call the behaviors we want to work on increasing or decreasing our "target behaviors"). Next, we need to break it down into baby steps!

Examples
•   With the goal of reading one book per month, baby steps include: getting a library card, finding a local discount bookstore, find a reading nook in your house or a local coffee shop that you could read in, set up a reward chart.
•   With the goal of visiting all national parks, baby steps include print out a list of all National Parks, begin to group them into regions, break it down by drivable trips and air travel trips, create a mock schedule of trips over the next 10 years.
•   With the goal of gratitude journaling, baby steps include finding a journal and pens you like, blocking out time to reflect each day, create a reward system for yourself.
Here are my baby steps:

1. _____

2. _____

3. _____

4. _____

5. _____

Great job!!! I am so proud of you for working though this; I am sure it was difficult. This is an example of doing the hard work and delaying gratification to meet your long-term goals.

One baby step I can tackle_____

_____

_____

Aim for one step per week!

GOALS THAT ARE WORTH REACHING TAKE WORK. HARD WORK.

Learning to "adult" means learning to identify your realistic long-term goals AND taking action to reach said goals! These goals need to align with your values and be achievable. We then need to use DBT® skills to tolerate the discomfort and pain along the way to achieving the goals. It reminds me of being on a road trip and having temptation at each exit. You must decide what is most important to you, date and time of arrival or having unique experiences along the way? If you value your schedule, you will need to use skills to keep your car on the highway. You will need to avoid the temptations of foods, coffee, and roadside attractions. On the other hand, if you value having unique and rich experiences it would be advisable to stop and see the world's largest ball of twine!

Now that we understand what adulting is, what is required, and the preliminary steps on the journey, we need to explore what gets in the way.

Which of the following are reasons that you choose to avoid adulting?

- Strong emotions
- Genuine confusion regarding tasks
- Giving into short term urges
- Fear of setting long term goals.
- Specific people _____
- Not sure how (to adult)
- No time
- Not enough money
- Tired
- Other _____

Skill: Willingness

It is quite possible that the reasons you have highlighted are completely valid! It is NOT a part of adulting well, however, to give up. One skill we need here is willingness. Willingness is the mindset that you will continue to choose to take paths on your journey despite any of the above roadblocks. To be willing requires a complete attitude adjustment, a shift away from catastrophic and/or pessimistic thought patterns, and a shift toward curious and optimistic problem solving. To be willing is NOT being stubborn or rigid.

Skill practice: Willingness
In what ways do you experience being stubborn?

Body sensations (heavy, fidgety, invigorated, hot, queasy)

_____

Thought patterns (racing, blank, negative)

_____

Behaviors (arms crossed, slumped, aggression, shutting down, silence)

_____

In what areas of life do you find yourself being more stubborn?

_____

_____

_____

In what ways do you stay stuck or suffer because of being stubborn?

_____

_____

_____

In what ways do you experience willingness?"
Body sensations (alert, weightless, fidgety, light/heavy)

_____

Thought patterns (racing, blank, negative/positive, optimistic,

calculated)

Behaviors (posture changes, approving/avoiding, talking more/less,

encouraging self or others)

_____

In what areas do you find yourself being more willing?

_____

_____

_____

In what ways do experience success because of being willing?

_____

_____

_____

Consider for a moment which of the adulting tasks you could commit to being more willing with Be specific. (ex: I will be more willing to open my bills and create a budget, more willing to attend family functions without pessimism, more willing to go to the gym)

1. _____

2. _____

3. _____

Part Two: The Grind

4 PASSING TIME

Let's do an experiment. What would you say if I asked, "how are you?"
My hypothesis is that one of your top three answers is "busy."
In a TED talk by Laura Vandercam in 2017 on time management, she gets real and does the math for us:

"There are 168 hours in a week. Twenty-four times seven is 168 hours. That is a lot of time. If you are working a full-time job, so 40 hours a week, sleeping eight hours a night, so 56 hours a week-- that leaves 72 hours for other things. That is a lot of time. You say you are working 50 hours a week, maybe a main job and a side hustle. Well, that leaves 62 hours for other things. You say you are working 60 hours. Well, that leaves 52 hours for other things ..."

Did you know that you have a choice in how you spend your time? We all tend to feel so OBLIGATED to do certain things: work, attend family functions, keep up with the news, put our kids in eight activities at any given time ...the REALITY is that we do what we make time for. We make time for what we believe is important– that can either mean what we value OR it can mean what we feel is expected of us. I want to teach you to find the dialectic and take more of a both/and approach, rather than an either/or approach. For example:

Going to work and working hard is a value of mine. Spending time with my family is also a value of mine. I prioritize them both; it is not an either/or. Sometimes this means I take a day off to spend time with my family. Sometimes it means that I take my kids to work with me. Sometimes it means I work long hours with intense focus. There is no right answer; however, there is an answer that supports your values and leaves you with less regret.

Mindfulness

Before we go any further into this book or the topic of time management, I must introduce mindfulness to you. As previously mentioned, it would be helpful if you have or are working through the Linehan Skills Training book also. Mindfulness is not a new concept from the world of DBT® and it is certainly not foreign in pop-culture. Mindfulness is presented in all therapies and all organized religions in one way or another. The only problem is that upon mentioning mindfulness, I tend to get resistance and people let their eyes glaze over while their ears close. Please do not do that! Mindfulness is THE key to freedom! Most people seek out mindfulness and/or meditation as a tool for generally selfish – I mean this in a great way, meaning that you are trying to improve or benefit yourself. Reasons people meditate:

- To find peace
- To become enlightened
- Experience a special state
- To get answers to questions
- Clarity
- Reduce pain
- Break habits
- The great news is that all of those will happen …the interesting news is that most people continue mindfulness/meditation for selfless reasons:
- They find themselves becoming more compassionate.
- They learn that they are able to fully give their attention to another.
- Their relationships improve, and people want to be nearer to them.

Mindfulness is when you decide what you will focus your attention on, with a curious openness and a sense of non-attachment. This means that you stop letting your thoughts boss you around! When you notice you are ruminating or focusing on negatives, you have a CHOICE! You can say to yourself "I notice that my mind has gone down that path again. I am going to bring my attention back to this moment, back to my breath". When you are "down that path" again (whatever that path may be), you are suffering. Suffering can be as simple as trying to plan your day while brushing your teeth or it can be utter panic while you are trying to function at work. Suffering is relative to the one moment you are in. Mindfulness lets you know that you do not have to suffer and frees you from unhelpful thinking patterns. We (therapists) frequently mention focusing on your breath (insert eye roll). The idea behind this is that if you are conscious/alive/awake, your breath is with you. This may be grim; however, if we instruct you to focus your attention on your pinky finger and then it gets cut off, you are back at square one! If we tell you that you can only calm down while looking at a fish in a fish tank, what are you supposed to do while panicking at the grocery store? If you are training yourself that you can only be calm with your teddy bear, what will you do at work? We must accept the fact that nothing is guaranteed to be accessible to us in a moment of crisis, except for our breathing.

A simple way to practice mindfulness is to sit in what I refer to as "wide awake posture" (sitting upright, if in a chair place both feet on the floor, shoulders relaxed and pleasant facial expression) and take 10 slow deep breaths. In those few minutes, all I want you to focus on is what it feels like for the breath to come into your nostrils, fill your lungs and diaphragm, and then slowly exit your body. Do this twice per day until it comes naturally, this practice will allow space for you to learn how to relate to your emotions differently. After time, with practice and consistency, simply breathing will become a calming and centering activity (when you choose to focus on your breath). In that way, you will habituate yourself to get the same result from one breath or ten breaths. Note: many people find it difficult to focus on breathing as it raises their anxiety to take a task from autonomic to conscious. For these people, it is important not to put restrictions (such as counting) on the breathing task, rather to instead just feel the breath as it comes in or out. If that is still too overwhelming, start with a focus on the soles of the feet, while continually trying the breathing periodically.

If you need other mindfulness ideas, there are an infinite number on the internet and there is an abundance of books on the topic. All religions incorporate mindfulness (be it through praying a rosary, reflective silence, worship music, or chanting) and most therapy tasks are intended to be done as a mindfulness practice. Common therapy recommendations for mindfulness include hiking, exercising, drinking hot tea, meditating, yoga, or listening to guided imagery. Remember, these things only count as a mindfulness practice if you do them with your full attention. When your mind wanders (and it will), you simply acknowledge that it has wandered and bring it back. It really is that simple; unfortunately, it is not always that easy. Here is a time where doing the hard work pays off. Let me share a real example from my life. A cohort of mine always shared how mindful hand washing was something that he had trained his body to use as a way to find his center. It sounded overly simple to me; however, as I will not preach what I do not practice, I decided to give it a try. It probably took me a month to remember to mindfully wash my hands. I would enter the bathroom with every intention of being fully present with the experience of hand washing …and then as I was drying my hands, I would realize I forgot to pay attention! After I finally got myself to pay attention, I practiced really noticing the sensation of the slippery soap as I washed my hands. I did this for about a month and I was really noticing that every time I washed my hands, my attention was PULLED toward noticing the soap and it was such a centering and calming experience. Fast forward another few weeks and I was navigating the hallways of the hospital toward the NICU to pick up my two-week-old five-pound daughter. I was a mess of emotions! I promise that zero percent of my attention was thinking about mindfulness. As I lugged the diaper bag, car seat, and my rubbery body though the first set of NICU doors, I remembered that I could not go through the second set of doors until I washed my hands in the supervised sink. Again, zero percent of me was thinking about mindfulness. And yet, I cannot put words to the sense of calm that came over me as I rubbed the soap between my hands! I was instantly calm and had a sense of clarity. I attribute that to the fact that I had done the hard work to condition myself to experience a sense of calm balance every time I washed my hands. I could have just given up that first month when I couldn't seem to remember to wash them mindfully. I could have said "it doesn't work" but I didn't! To say it did not work would have been a fallacy as the only reason it didn't work in that first month was because I wasn't doing it! Please remember this story as you have urges to give up on mindfulness. It is the foundation of all skills because all skills must be done mindfully if you want them to work. For each person, a mindfulness practice may need to be "tweaked" to be most effective for you (such as focusing on the scent of the soap vs the texture, or the temperature of the water vs the soap); listen to your gut and change it as you see fit. The results are worth it though, that alone is a reason to start practicing NOW!

States of Mind

Within mindfulness, DBT® also asks that you understand that we all have two distinct states of mind and our goal is to reach "wise mind," which is the synthesis of the two. In DBT® the states of mind are captured in a Venn diagram as pictured on the next page:

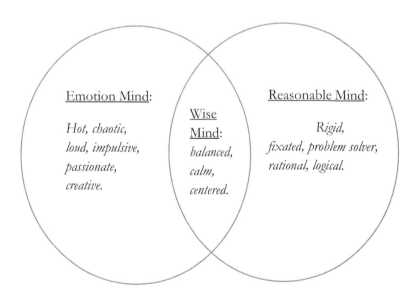

Emotion Mind:

Hot, chaotic, loud, impulsive, passionate, creative.

Wise Mind:

balanced, calm, centered.

Reasonable Mind:

Rigid, fixated, problem solver, rational, logical.

Emotion mind is a loud, chaotic, emotion driven state. It is often categorized as hot, chaotic, extreme, and passionate; can result in impulsive actions; makes it difficult to think logically; it is a mindset in which we find it easier to distort facts, reality, and perceptions. In emotion mind, you are not always seeing things clearly and can make regrettable choices. Other DBT® modalities call it "fatalistic mind" (the sky is falling!) or "being" mind (as you are so caught up with being in the moment that you may miss things). One risk of emotion-minded decisions can result from the accompanying sense of urgency. You forget to think through all potential consequences. While often looked at as a bad thing, there are beneficial and socially acceptable times to be in emotion mind: concerts, social gatherings, funerals, performances, while creating art. Emotion mind is passionate, spontaneous, artistic, creative, and empathetic. The reality is, without emotion minded people, change would not occur in legislation and we wound not have performance or visual arts!

Reasonable mind is a logic and fact-based way of thinking. Feelings are not terribly important when you are in reasonable mind, which can lead to unintentionally hurting people's feelings. In reasonable mind, you may be analytical and rigid in thought patterns. People in reasonable mind are often seen as cold or unfeeling because they are primarily focused on facts, rules, and logic. While emotion-minded people would describe reasonable mind as "boring," it can be a great asset when you are working on your budget, following a complex recipe, or trying to learn new skills! The fantastic attributes of reasonable mind are that it can help you learn skills and understand when to apply them; it helps you store and decode information and is the type of thinking that drives problem solving.

When in the extremes of either reasonable or emotional mind, we will ignore particularly important factors. The goal in this book is to look at how you feel about something AND consider what you know about something prior to making a decision. Wise mind is our goal. It is where you take what you know and how you feel about a situation and you make the best decision for yourself. The active integration of reasonable mind and emotional mind leads us to wise mind. We know we are operating from wise mind when we experience a calm, quietness about the situation. It is seeing and responding to "what is" instead of what we want, or what we think "should" be. Wise mind holds in awareness the interconnectedness of life, instead of the selfish nature of emotion mind or the insensitive nature of reasonable mind. I like to remember that wise mind can wait (that would make a great bumper sticker)!

Remember, there are no *right* answers in life; however, there are choices that support your own values and help you achieve your long-term goals. The kicker here is that I passionately believe that everyone has a wise mind; that means that your wise mind might tell you to do something DIFFERENT than my own. That does not make one of us wrong. The effective choice for you may not be the effective choice for me, and vice versa. While emotion mind has a sense of urgency, wise mind has a sense of calm patience. Wise mind knows that it can wait. Emotion mind will try to convince you to REACT; ...wise mind will help you learn to RESPOND skillfully and therefore increase the odds that you reach your long-term goals. Wise mind also requires you to embrace change and an experimental nature; as this does not come naturally, you will need to try out new and different ideas!

Example: in marriage, your long-term goal is (usually) to stay married. When you are emotional; however, emotion mind will say DIVORCE when dishes aren't done, DIVORCE with every disagreement, DIVORCE at first financial problem. Reasonable mind will say DIVORCE because they fold the towels "wrong" or they balance the budget "wrong"! Slowing down and getting into wise mind will help you to have a respectful discussion without resorting to either extreme. You will need to pull in the afore mentioned skills of dialectics and validation.

Skill: States of Mind

Fill in your experience of the three states of mind. What words, experiences, sensations, and urges do you experience in emotion, wise, and reasonable minds?

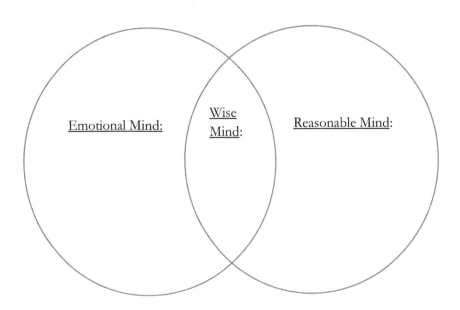

Emotional Mind:

Wise Mind:

Reasonable Mind:

Mindfulness and Time

I hope you are beginning to see how the two ideas, mindfulness, and time, are connected.

When we are not mindful, we become slave to whatever emotional urge we have in that moment. We can lose track of time by allowing ourselves to be all-consumed by ineffective thoughts. Mindfulness teaches us to slow down and generate awareness of what is happening in our lives. Mindfulness allows us to plan for each day and prioritize what order to attack the task list. It also allows us to stop when a distraction arises and make a conscious decision about whether to attend to the distraction or stick to the plan.

An example of this is when we are working (homework, bills at home, at our place of employment) and someone comes into our space with a crisis. We can learn to pause the conversation or ask for a moment so that we can decide which task should be attended to next. We use emotions AND logic to make that decision. If we always follow emotion, we will jump down every rabbit hole and we will not get very much done. If we always follow logic, we might lose and damage relationships along the way. Again, there is no right answer; there is an effective choice we can make to best meet our long-term goals and to prioritize two competing long-term goals (such as keeping your job and keeping your best friend).

I was recently contemplating my life and the disparity between what I would like to do and what I actually do. The main excuse I provide myself (usually as a rationalization), is that I do not have time. The most frequent example that comes to mind is going to the gym. So often I wake up early, get off work early, or generally have a few hours on the weekend in which I think "I should go to the gym." I know (reasonable mind) that going to the gym improves my mood, increases my confidence and sense of mastery; however, I typically talk myself OUT of going for a variety of emotion-based reasons. The act of talking myself out of going leaves me feeling lazy, defeated, and hypocritical (emotion mind). I don't know about you, but I'd chose accomplished and proud over sluggish any day (and yet I don't). The thing is, I always have time. Even if it's 15 minutes, I could do some free weights and not need a shower. If it's an hour, I could get in a really "good" workout. The trick is acting from a goal-oriented state of mind rather than from current emotion. The action you take, and your urges can exist independently from one another.

Other things I would like to do are read more, go to parks, call friends and relatives, and paint. I know from experience that it is not as easy as "just do it"; and yet it is! I often remind others that skillful behavior is "simple, not easy". Once I start doing any of these things, the ball is rolling and I am more likely to follow through with the task. For example, if the phone is already ringing, I am not going to hang up on my dear aunt! If I'm already in the car with my dog, I am not likely to turn around and go back home, and if I turn off the TV/radio and open a book, I am more likely to actually read a chapter. Action begets action.

The message I am trying to convey is that you (and I) need to peel apart our emotions from our actions. Scheduling allows us to find time for what we need to do and what we want to do in a week, and then we must find ways to reinforce the behavior by rewarding ourselves for a job well done!

Time Tracking

Time tracking is a skill I suggest you use to achieve the above-mentioned goal. It is where you audit your use of time for several weeks. It is crucial to be non-judgmental and curious during this process. I have found that as I do this, I tend to be embarrassed at how much time I "waste" by watching TV, and my emotional urge is to stop tracking. It is imperative to get an accurate look at where your time is going if you want to be able to make changes. This is another example of doing the hard work and experiencing short-term discomfort in an effort to achieve long-term success. I challenge you to use this grid (make copies as needed) and track what you are spending your time on for at least two weeks. Some people find it helpful to color code the blocks at the end of each week (i.e., time at work = green, pleasure time = yellow, eating = blue, time on electronics = orange).

Once you have your snapshot and can calculate averages (on average a person might spend 41 hours per week working, 10 hours per week driving, 9 hours per week watching television) you can start to explore whether you are spending time in a way that helps you reach your goals, feel competent and maintain your self-respect. I would venture to say that there is something about your time audit that you will feel some embarrassment or frustration with. It could be that you spend too much time at work and not enough time with your family. It could be that you spend more time in the car than you would like. It could be that you spend more time eating than you would like. Please resist the urge to make excuses and/or minimize the truth.

The idea here is to review your long-term goals and your values. Follow the worksheet after the time audit log to make some decisions that will improve your identity, improve your self-worth and self-respect. Remember, there is nothing wrong with downtime. I believe it is 100% necessary– what you need to look at are the ratios/trends that you see in your time use and the emotional result of how you spend your time.

Time Tracking Log
Week of:

Time	Sun	Mon		Tues	Wed	Thurs	Fri	Sat
6am								
7am								
8am								
9am								
10am								
11am								
12pm								
1pm								
2pm								
3pm								
4pm								
5pm								

6pm								
7pm								
8pm								
9pm								
11pm								

Fill in each block with the general idea of what you were doing during that hour.

Observations from time log

What are the top five categories that you spend time on? What are the most common associated emotions?

Example:

1.   *Work — this makes me feel accomplished, helpful, productive, tired, and sometimes angry.*

2.   *Driving — this makes me feel sad, unproductive, stressed, and wasteful.*

3.   *"Down" time (tv/electronics) — this makes me feel embarrassed and lazy.*

4.   *Family activities — this makes me feel proud, connected, loved, and sad that it's fourth.*

5.   *Church — this makes me feel content.*

1. _____

2. _____

3. _____

4. _____

5. _____

Take some time to journal on the questions listed below:

Review your values and long term-goals before moving on. What are some values you could work on supporting with minor changes in how you spend your time?

Based on your observations of the time log and review of your values assessment, what changes could you make to improve your self-worth, self-esteem and overall feelings of confidence and enjoyment?

Example: I could work on being mindful while at work and having a more positive attitude of my productivity and ability to support my family financially. I could work on having a better attitude in the car by listening to upbeat music or feeling productive in the car by listening to audiobooks. I could work to transfer some of time spent on electronics to being time spent with family.

What emotions do you think you would feel if you worked toward implementing at least one of those changes?

Example*: pride, happier and more productive*

Cues:

I mentioned in my handwashing example that it took me over one month to remember to wash my hands mindfully. I could have sped up that process if I implemented the use of a cue. According to Merriam Webster dictionary, a cue is "a signal (such as a word, phrase, or bit of stage business) to a performer to begin a specific speech or action" or "something serving a comparable purpose (ex: I'll take that yawn as my cue to leave). As behaviorists, we know that we need to use classical conditioning to increase the likelihood that we will repeat a desired behavior. Using these two ideas, we can see how a cue to wash my hands mindfully could have trained me faster. A cue in this scenario could be a specific (and unique) soap, a sign on the mirror or an alarm on my phone. Anything that reminds us to take a desired action can be a cue. Over time, feeling the slipperiness of the soap while handwashing became my cue to be mindful and present.

If you are looking for a cue to spend more time with your family, you could change the backdrop of your cell phone or electronic (if these are the items that distract you) to a picture of your family. You could put a chart up on the refrigerator in which you give yourself a sticker for each night you spend time as a family. In that scenario, the chart is the cue, while the sticker is a positive reinforcer. If you are looking for a cue to drink more water, you could wear your bracelet or watch on the "wrong" wrist. Each time you want to switch it or question why it is there, you remind yourself to take a drink of water. When I am looking for inspiration for new and creative cues, I find boutique and craft stores to be a great resource! They have aisle after aisle of inexpensive and/or unique items that can be used to remind you and motivate you to change your mindset.

Skill: Pros/cons

Pros and cons are an essential tool for making tough decisions. I can tell you that I use the pros and cons skill to make time management decisions all the time! It is not an easy choice to decide whether to work longer hours while kids are in daycare or whether to attend a family event when it interferes with another scheduled task.

Pros and cons, done the DBT® way, look different than the traditional two-column T-chart that you are likely familiar with. In addition to exploring the pros of doing _____ and the cons of doing _____, we also stretch the brain by adding two more rows at the bottom and exploring the pros of not doing _____ and the cons of not doing _____ (yes that is a double negative; while complicated, it seems to allow me to think differently and come up with different answers). Examples and practice will follow.

Pros and cons should be done from all states of mind to capture all thoughts. Including emotion minded reasons and reasonable (stubborn) reasons can give valid insight into a situation. Can you imagine what kind of pros you could come up with for quitting your job if you were in emotion mind?! Emotion minded answers can absolutely be included; however, if done correctly and over time, the pros and cons chart should also include reasonable minded and wise minded answers. Can you also think of reasonable reasons to quit your job? Both emotion-minded and reasonable-minded reasons can bring to light things that are important and should be explored. I encourage you to take your pros and cons chart with you; work on it over the course of at least 7 days. The size of the decisions will increase the number of days you work on it. Remember, wise mind reminds you that you can wait. If you are feeling a sense of urgency, you are likely in emotional mind or even in reasonable mind.

Skill Practice: Pros and cons

	Pros		Cons
Of ___ ___ ___			
Of not ___ ___ ___			

I encourage you to copy this page or re-draw it in your journal. Come back to the chart often over the week and add as many points as you can, no matter how silly or serious the ideas are. The goal is not to count the items and say that the box with the most items wins; rather, pay attention to the weight each item carries for you. One wise-minded idea could very well outweigh ten emotion-minded ideas.

Skill: Self-encouragement

The last skill I want to introduce in this chapter is the skill of self-encouragement (which you will find nestled in the DBT® acronym of IMPROVE, further explained in chapter eight). I am astounded at how hard people are on themselves compared to how gentle and forgiving they can be of others. The basic premise here is that your internal dialogue needs to be in alignment with how you would speak to a friend. When a friend comes to you with a struggle, I would venture to believe that you are supportive, encouraging, validating, and nurturing. Take those four qualities and start using them on yourself! How many times have you have sat, paralyzed, ruminating about your to-do list? Have you found yourself being so overwhelmed that you cannot possibly even think through what the first step could be? We call this "analysis-paralysis" in therapy. When your productivity is stalled, your self-esteem typically tanks. When your self-esteem tanks, your productivity will plummet. When your productivity plummets, you are likely to experience depression and/or anxiety. I think we can see the problem here.

Self-encouragement is necessary for time management because you WILL make mistakes, become overwhelmed and confused! You will make choices that you regret. These might include low productivity at work because of getting sucked into a co-worker's drama, not reading as much as your values would suggest, not going to the gym despite physical health being a priority, or not going to bed at a reasonable time. When those things happen (not if- - when...) I ask that you give yourself grace and encourage yourself into change, rather than belittling or trying to abuse yourself into change. Guess what, the latter does not work! If it did ...you would not be reading this book!

The way you speak to yourself will either improve your emotional wellbeing or cause you to spiral downward. Self-encouragement means that you speak to yourself as you would speak to a friend, to a child, to a loved one. If you make a mistake (as you will), you say to yourself, "That's ok, I have learned from this and now I know how to do it differently next time" or "Just because I made a mistake, does not make me a mistake" or "Mistakes happen and are a part of growth. I am so proud of my effort and courage to try." Self-encouragement means that you stop judging yourself and start forgiving yourself.

We have already identified how self-judgment stalls productivity. When you find yourself overwhelmed by your to-do list, encouraging and being kind to yourself can free you from the cycle of rumination. What I suggest is that you start each day with some positive affirmations. Before you get out of bed, tell yourself that you believe in yourself, that you believe you are worthy, and that you have faith in yourself.

Other ideas to surround yourself with self-encouragement cues:
- Make a Pinterest board of encouraging quotes.
- Create a collage that captures your intentions.
- Write quotes or encouraging statements on your mirrors with dry-erase marker.
- Purchase some items that have encouraging statements on them.
- Print out those encouraging phrases and post in your environment.
- Follow inspirational people on social media.
- Splurge on that wall art that moves you.
- Set the backdrop of your phone and/or laptop to be motivational.
- Use bathtub crayons in your shower to remind you to be kind to yourself.
- Buy a positive thought-a-day calendar.
- Buy jewelry with inspirational/calming/encouraging phrases on it.

Skill Practice: Self-Encouragement

Encouraging statements that I would say to a friend who was struggling with guilt over a decision or negative emotions about themselves:

Example: *Take it easy; you aren't perfect, and I can tell that you are trying. What can I do to support you in making it to the gym in the next seven days? You are so important to me.*

_____

_____

_____

Take those statements and reframe them into self-statements:

Example: *Take it easy, I am not perfect, and I can tell that I am trying. What or who could be helpful to support me in making it to the gym in the next seven days?*

_____

_____

_____

Please note, the statements can be effective if unaltered from their friend-encouraging state. That means you have less of an excuse not to use this skill! Be your own friend, not your own enemy! You can take a dry-erase marker and write one of your self-encouraging messages on your mirror or post the statement on your desk at work …anywhere you will see it! Really consider buying yourself those t-shirts, mugs, wall art, calendars, etc. that you would buy a friend. You are worth it! (Say that out loud …" I am worth it!")

5 MONEY CAN'T BUY HAPPINESS...

I am going to go there. I am going to talk about that which no one talks about! We are going to talk about and look at money. If your urge is to close the book and say "NO WAY!" I'd venture to say you need to keep reading! If your urge is to be excited because you love a good spreadsheet, I would venture to say you need to keep reading! As I said before, this book is for everyone. Dialectical thinking is necessary for everyone. It is essential to continue to look at both sides of each situation. For example: looking at how money is a reward and how money is a responsibility. You must remember that there is no "right" way to do something; rather, there are more effective choices along the way that will help you reach your goals!

What I see when I bring up the big M (money) in therapy is the following problems arise: avoidance, anxiety, ignorance, and pessimism. We are going to unpack and break down each one.

Avoidance

All problematic behaviors (in any area of life) are an effort at avoidance. When we reach for our problem behavior in a frantic effort to distract, we create new problems! The same is true with avoidant money behaviors, such as:

- avoiding making a budget
- avoiding talking to your family/significant other or yourself about the realities of your finances
- avoiding creating and using a shopping list
- avoiding checking your balances
- avoiding opening bills and/or paying bills
- avoiding meal planning (food is one of the most common categories for overspending)
- avoiding education on topics surrounding money

A common example of avoidance: television. I have not had network television or cable TV in over 7 years. I do not miss it, nor do I feel as though I am MISSING OUT on anything. For 4 of those 7 years, I didn't even have a television on the main floor of my home. I do not have a television in my bedroom. Nope, not missing it AT ALL! If you think of what you are doing when you are watching TV, the answer is typically some sort of avoidance. Avoiding housework, avoiding homework, avoiding sleep, avoiding your significant other, etc. ...you are also avoiding more effective behaviors: going for a walk, exercising, painting, reading, talking to a friend ...We must confront avoidance as it relates to finances.

If you compare the items from those two collections, I would venture to bet that if you choose an avoidance activity, you will feel worse: more depressed, sluggish, unmotivated, lonely, sad, etc. As a result of choosing an effective activity, I'd bet you feel better: accomplished, productive, proud, happy, relieved, connected. On any given day, during any given moment, which would you choose ...to feel unmotivated and depressed or to feel productive and happy? Framing it in this way makes it seem silly to choose avoidance. I do believe that is a simple (not easy) choice, and yet many of us choose to feel more sluggish and dejected by binge watching shows by the season! There are many ways to achieve decreased TV watching (limit yourself, decrease channels paid for, join a gym), but how have those worked for you so far? My ideas of only owning ONE television, not having cable or network TV, and not having a TV in your bedroom do put a barrier into place that reduce the likelihood of watching to excess. Do I still binge-watch Netflix sometimes? Yes. Does it make me feel sluggish, unmotivated, and depressed? Almost every time! But I watch so much less TV than I ever have in my life ...and that makes me HAPPY, PROUD, and PRODUCTIVE! This fits into the framework of financial decisions as well. When we choose to sign up for too many monthly services, avoid opening bills, refuse to learn about financial matters, we will end up feeling lousy! Even though it is hard, we need to make choices from the effective action column!

The good news is that almost every skill I present, regardless of which chapter it falls in or in what context it is presented, can be used to treat your avoidance behaviors. For example, you have already learned: pros and cons, mindfulness, acceptance vs change, long-term goals setting, values assessment, states of mind, and self-encouragement. Every single one of these skills is necessary when tackling financial woes. Take some time now to re-practice the skills, specifically related to money.

Skill Practice: Pros and Cons

	Pros	Cons
Of using a budget		
Of not using a budget		

As I mentioned before, I encourage you to re-draw this template into your journal (with much bigger squares) and complete a pros and cons on the idea of making a budget, or on the idea of educating yourself more about financial topics, on being more honest about your financial situation, etc. Do one on each topic you are struggling with.

Skill Practice: States of Mind

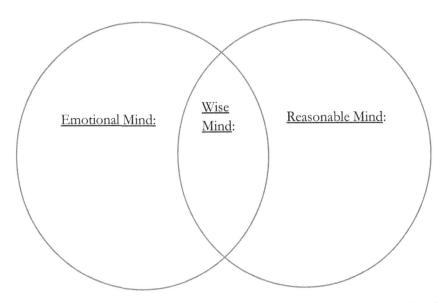

Take a moment to fill in the states of mind circles with your emotional experience surrounding money.

• What does emotion mind tell you about money? What urges do you have? What types of thinking patterns do you notice in emotion mind?

• What does reasonable mind tell you about money? What urges do you have? What types of thinking patterns do you notice in reasonable mind?

• What does wise mind tell you about money? What urges do you have? What types of thinking patterns do you notice in wise mind?

Now take a minute to consider what you could do to get into wise mind, prior to working on the rest of this chapter, prior to working on a budget. Is there a cue that you could use to remind yourself? (i.e., a sticker on your debit/credit card, beach scene checks, an alarm in your phone to meditate on each payday?) This is where you can harness the power of mindfulness to see change in your life! Turn back to your values assessment and check to see if your wise mind urges are in line with your long-term value-based goals.

Anxiety

Did you know that the opossum "plays dead" or has "apparent death" when it perceives attack? This can include complete physical paralysis for a period of time! Anxiety surrounding money is quite common. It leads us to "play dead", so to speak, by completely ignoring our bank accounts or finances. The unfortunate thing about this reaction to money is that if you play dead/avoid, you WILL suffer. I will admit that this is one of my defaults! When I do not like where my bank account balance is, I am much more likely to avoid checking it ...leading to almost certain overdrawing! This is a self-punishing choice, and I can tell you, it NEVER works. The antidote of anxiety is to approach, rather than avoid.

Some skills you can use to address this problem include cope ahead and paced breathing.

Skill: Cope Ahead

Cope ahead is a skill to use when you are having recurrent fears of possible future events. Cope ahead treats anxiety because it exposes you to the feared situation in a safe setting (your mind). You would practice coping ahead when the feared event is NOT happening. The steps are as follows:

1. Describe the feared event factually.

We know that describing something factually will already decrease your heightened emotional state (i.e., "what if I lose my job and I cannot support my family and I have to move into my parent's basement?" will cause increased anxiety. "I am worried about how I would cope if I lost my job" is much less catastrophic and more of a tangible problem to be solved).

2. Decide which skills you could use to problem solve or cope with the feared situation.

This allows you to "go there" without having to live through it or lie awake in paralyzing anxiety each night. This step is about being curious and wondering what skills you could try. I encourage you to practice this in the morning, when you have the mental energy needed without triggering a meltdown. Waiting until the evening can result in target behaviors. (i.e., if I lost my job, I would start putting in applications right away. I would slow my spending by not going out to eat or buying clothing. I would accept an undesired job as a stepping stone toward a better fit. I would be sure to use encouraging self-talk and take care of what is in my control: sleeping, eating well, and exercising.

3. Envision the experience actually happening and practice coping well.

This means allowing your anxiety to rise and fall as you are visualizing the experience. This will allow you to build a sense of accomplishment and mastery over your fears. You will show yourself that you CAN cope well, that you DO know how to problem solve. It is also necessary to practice rewarding yourself after coping well within the imagery so that you remember to reward yourself after coping well with the actual event! Cope ahead teaches you to practice coping well and praising your own efforts instead of panicking and then beating yourself up afterward.

It is a truth that what you practice in your head is more likely to happen. This is why you were probably taught to practice a speech in a mirror PRIOR to delivering to a crowd! This theory works well with money, too. I cannot tell you how many people have said things like, "I just don't understand retirement, so I don't think about it." Or "I know there isn't enough money for everything, so I don't make a budget." The problem with this strategy is that it ensures future problems! Cope ahead encourages you to go through the steps and visualize handling scheduling and attending a meeting with a financial advisor with confidence. Visualize yourself asking questions and doing slow, deep breathing. Cope ahead would encourage you to rehearse mentally what you would do to cope with the anxieties and frustrations of making a budget when money is tight. Coping ahead is like a fire drill in schools. It is not about planning and worrying about HOW the fire started ...it is about recognizing that there is a fire and coping well by efficiently escaping the building!

Skill Practice: Cope Ahead
   List your top financial fears:

1. _____

2. _____

3. _____

4. _____

5. _____

Follow the steps below and practice coping ahead on each event. Record in your journal.

Step 1: Describe the fear factually.

Step 2: Describe which skills you will try to cope effectively and/or problem solve the event.

Step 3: Imagine coping well and getting through the event with more ease than you fear.

Step 4: Practice calming and regulating yourself.

Ignorance

Ignorance is likely the perfect word for me in some financial areas. I do not mean ignorance to be heard in the stigmatized way that I fear you will hear it. Ignorant does not mean stupid. It means that you are un-educated in an area. For example: I am ignorant to the ins-and-outs of retirement planning. I have a basic understanding; however, it is not something that I have spent a lot of time researching. I rely on other professionals to help me make decisions in this area.

I used to be ignorant in most topics related to finances. I used mindfulness skills to become aware of this, to wake up to my reality. I then used wise mind to decide that I wanted to become more knowledgeable. I did the pros and cons of several programs and ultimately decided to attend Dave Ramsey's Financial Peace University. I found Dave Ramsey to be a behaviorist, and quite "DBT®" in his approach. I appreciate his *tell it like it is* mentality while also breaking it down in ways that my uninformed brain could comprehend! I recommend this program if you can find one in your area. Look at http://www.daveramsey.com/fpu for local classes or to sign up for on-line classes.

Three skills that will add to your repertoire to use toward conquering ignorance with money are: willingness, radical acceptance and turning the mind. These three skills are taught in the distress tolerance module of DBT ...seems fitting considering how much money can send us into a spiral!

Willingness

Willingness (also discussed in previous chapters) is a skill that alludes to the benefit of you being a WILLING participant in your finances and stop being a stubborn ostrich with its head in the sand. I believe it is a difficult concept to use in real life; therefor I will review it many times throughout the text. Willingness means that you are prepared to do what is necessary to make change and be effective. Willingness applies in all arenas of life; however, in the realm of money, willingness means you stop avoiding and start budgeting! Willingness may also require you to seek counsel from a financial professional!

Willingness in general means that you make a conscious choice to participate in the world, playing by the rules of the world even though they are not as you wish they were. Because willingness is a choice, you must embrace it with your entire body if you want the full effect. This means a willing posture and facial expressions. Willing posture includes uncrossing legs and arms and opening palms up; willing facial expression includes a relaxed jaw and forehead with gentle eyes. Your body language communicates to your brain chemistry and will help ease up any resistance you are feeling; I will teach you more on this in Chapter 8.

When I think of willingness, I like to remember what it is like to play a board game with a child. When children start to fall behind, they tend to pout and refuse to play. They are not very willing to continue; it is not very fun to play with this child. The same idea is true in adulting: if you are falling behind, pouting, and refusing will not help you ...in fact, it may reduce the likelihood that anyone will be willing to help you. No one wants to play cards with a sore loser.

Skill Practice: Willingness

Would you say that you are stubborn in the realm of money? Do you often struggle to tell yourself "no" related to a short-term goal (*it's on sale!*) in order to achieve a long-term goal (*I want to save for a down payment on a home*)? Do you get frustrated when people try to give you advice on how to budget? Have you found yourself avoiding checking your bills or account balances? Have you been ostriching?

If you answered yes to any of these, you need to consider what changes would be possible if you were more willing to manage your money differently.

What are some goals with money and how willing are you to work on them (0-5)?

For Example: *I would like to save $6000 in my savings account (3)*

1. _____

2. _____

3. _____

4. _____

5. _____

What areas of your life would improve if you were willing to work toward these goals?

_____

_____

_____

_____

Radical Acceptance

Radical acceptance is one of the most difficult and LIFE CHANGING skills ...if you are willing to apply it! Radical acceptance requires that you already understand the benefits of willingness. You can use radical acceptance for almost anything that causes you distress but is a fact of the current world/your history/your current situation. As a skill, it is crucial to reaching your life worth living as it offers freedom from suffering by acknowledging what is, identifying where we have a choice, and therefore turning suffering into pain you can endure. In many ways, once you learn to apply radical acceptance it can be your best friend and can keep you from getting into more trouble. Radical acceptance does not require you to approve of or like the situation; rather, it requires you to wake up to the fact that at present, you cannot change the fact of the issue and that you want to stop being angry about it.

It requires …a lot of PRACTICE! As you will discover in this book, acceptance is not a concept that one grasps overnight. The idea behind acceptance can be generalized in the classic Serenity Prayer:

"God, grant me the serenity to accept the things I cannot change, the courage to change the things I can, and the wisdom to know the difference."

In DBT® lingo:

"Grant me the serenity to radically accept the things I cannot change, the courage to use the skills to change the things I can, and the wise mind to know the difference."

In life, there are a significant number of things that occur that we cannot change directly: weather, politics, other people's behaviors, our physical attributes/genetic traits, costs of items. Conversely, in our lives, there are a significant number of things we CAN change which are generally related to our behaviors/reactions/responses (which influence our emotions and thoughts). Dialectical behavioral therapy as a whole seeks to help individuals determine what is in their control and what is out of their control and then take the most effective action (either accept or change). I believe acceptance is so difficult because as a culture, we are pushed to things faster, bigger, stronger …more, more, more …thus giving the message that everything IS within our control. This leads to a very anxious society! Radical acceptance is the idea of playing the hand you were dealt (regardless of how crummy it is) instead of throwing a temper tantrum or refusing to play. Would you want to play cards with "Bob" who flipped the table every time he didn't like the cards that were dealt to him? Bob's behavior in the scenario would increase his suffering as people would surely stop playing with him and he would likely experience shame and become increasingly isolated. Do not flip the table on your own money management.

Acceptance requires clarity: the ability to discern what is legitimately in and out of our control. Acceptance is NOT to say that we will never change, it is NOT to say that we approve of it, and it is NOT to say that we like the situation. Acceptance is to say that we recognize that we no longer want to suffer because of fighting reality. The following are a few financial and non-financial examples:

Ex. 1: You were bullied in high school and you continue to re-live it, dredge up the memories, look the people up on social media, thus torturing yourself with the related thoughts.

Radical acceptance could include recognizing that you are continuing to keep those memories alive (this is not to say the actual bullying is your fault or that it is something you should not feel angry about), thus increasing your own suffering. Radical acceptance looks like admitting what happened and really allowing yourself to feel sad for your high-school self. You may need to disable your social media accounts as you are no longer going to allow those memories to rule your behaviors.

Ex. 2: You made poor financial choices in the past that have left you with debt and poor credit.

Radical acceptance could be that you recognize that you own your past choices and get honest with yourself about their present implications. Often when people are fighting reality, they continue to spend excessively and put more and more on lines of credit. Radical acceptance would challenge you to live as if you believed you were capable of financial control (have a budget, pay more than minimum balance, etc.). Radical acceptance means you are going to change your internal self-talk and cease beating yourself up about past choices as they cannot be changed, all the while empowering yourself and moving toward more effective money management.

Once you practice radical acceptance on smaller things: gas prices going up, weather, your paycheck size …then (and only then) you can begin practice radical acceptance on bigger and bigger things …all the way up to accepting past traumas. I suggest practice with a therapist because this is such a complex topic!

Radical acceptance has three main components:
1. What is the reality (fact) that you do not like?
2. What do you do because of your refusal to accept it?
3. How do YOU suffer as a result?

Ex. 1: *I don't like having to pay my regional taxes. As a result, I don't pay them! I suffer because in April, I am being sent letters that feel threatening and I owe more money to the local government than I feel that I can afford. They threaten to put a tax lien against me.*

Ex. 2: *It isn't fair that gas prices went up right when my tank hit empty. As a result, I don't get gas because I think I can make it to work "on empty." As a result, I suffer because I run out of gas, have to pay AAA, and I am late to work.*

Ex. 3: *Textbooks shouldn't cost hundreds of dollars per semester. As a result, I don't buy them because I think I can "just pay attention". As a result, I suffer because I remain angry at the professor with every low grade, I miss assignments that are in the book, and I might lose my scholarship due to low grades.*

Radical acceptance as a skill means that you have a frank conversation with yourself about what YOU are doing to contribute to YOUR suffering. It can be difficult to do this as it causes frustration, and many people feel blamed. I encourage you to see the freedom and choice in this skill rather than the blame. Once you realize that you have a choice in all matters, you realize that you can make things better or worse for yourself. I encourage you to make the most effective choice, even if it is frustrating. I do not disagree that many situations in life are not "fair." Fair is a four-letter "F" word; it will do little more than make you angry. I suggest you remove it from your vocabulary.

Skill: Radical Acceptance

Consider for a moment some facts about your life (or life in general) that you do not like:

1. _____

2. _____

3. _____

4. _____

5. _____

Next, I want you to honestly write what you do because of not wanting to accept the above facts (one line for each fact listed above):

1. _____

2. _____

3. _____

4. _____

5. _____

Thirdly, in what ways do YOU suffer as a result?

1. _____

2. _____

3. _____

4. _____

5. _____

Turning the Mind

Turning the mind is the close cousin skill of radical acceptance. One of the reasons people do not like hearing about acceptance is that it oversimplifies a complex and emotional experience. I often hear people lament, *"Don't you think if I could let it go, I would?!?."* I agree! *"Letting it go"* is often invalidating of the heaviness of the situation we are wrestling with. Sure, I can "let go" of the fact that the line around the coffee shop is too long to stop in, and I can "let go" of the fact that I didn't win the radio contest …BUT I CANNOT let go of _____! Remember …radical acceptance is less about "letting it go" and more about "letting it be." (A little more Beatles, a little less Elsa.) Turning the mind is the idea that for bigger issues, we need to turn toward acceptance: again, and again, and again. We might need to do this every 10 minutes in the beginning. Please trust that it will get easier and you will be able to expand that from every 10 minutes to every hour, then every day, and sometimes even weeks between recalling the upsetting life situation and needing to remind yourself to be effective by accepting it is as it is, not as you wish it would be.

Turning the mind is agreeing that you want to be less triggered or upset by X, Y, or Z reality in your life (past wrongs, current injustices, physical or emotional pain you have been experiencing). Turning the mind is an inner commitment to keep turning towards the path of acceptance each time you realize that you are down that rabbit hole again. Turning the mind is an inner choice to keep trying. Turning the mind means you are not giving up! Turning the mind requires a sense of willingness, that you are no longer slave to your urges (money urges or otherwise).

Skill: Turning the Mind

To use turning the mind, we must be mindfully aware of what it is that we are not accepting. Make a list of the things that you are struggling to accept related to your finances:

Example: *I do not like that I have student loans. It is not "fair," and I don't want to repay them.*

1. _____

2. _____

3. _____

4. _____

5. _____

Now take a moment to close your eyes and make an inner commitment to yourself. Commit to yourself that you will work to accept the above issues. As you are working on this commitment to yourself, I want you to be sure that you have calm/content posture and facial expressions, calm/content body language, and calm/content tone in your thoughts.

Ex: *I will pay $30 more than the minimum balance on my student loans each month on the 15th.*

Lastly, I want you to write an encouraging note to yourself that includes your plan for addressing the stubborn willfulness next time it pops up:

Dear me,

_____

_____

_____

_____

_____I

love you and you are worth it! Love, Me

Pessimism

The last area that we need to explore related to money struggles is the cognitive distortion known as pessimism. Being pessimistic can result from many things: your parents trained you to be pessimistic, you had several consecutive disappointments in life, you are fearful of dreaming that things can be better, or the state of our world politics! I view pessimism as a combination of cognitive distortions rolled together. To be truly pessimistic, one must have mastered over-generalization, catastrophic thinking patterns, personalizing, and disqualifying the positive.

According to David Burns MD in his book *Feeling Good: The New Mood Therapy*, the following definitions explain each cognitive distortion:

1. Overgeneralization – Seeing a single negative event as a never-ending pattern of defeat.

2. Catastrophic Thinking – Exaggerating the importance of things (such as a mistake you made)

3. Disqualifying the Positive – Rejecting positive experiences by insisting that they "don't count."

4. Personalizing – Seeing yourself as the cause of negative external events (that you really had no responsibility for)

Imagine that you have two radios playing, one on each side of your head (or headphones on with a different station playing in each ear). Ugh …how annoying would that be! I get so anxious when I am hearing two messages simultaneously when people are trying to talk over each other, or someone is trying to talk over the television/radio. This is, in many ways, what it is like inside of the head of someone struggling with cognitive distortions. One radio (typically the louder one) is shouting messages that are distorted by your experiences, society, or messages from past interactions: *"you aren't good enough," "why don't you give up," "why do you even try," "no one likes you," "you should stay home," "you are worthless,"* etc. The other radio or headphone is very quietly whispering one or two healthier thoughts: *"you can do this," "you are worth something," "people enjoy your company," "you are worthy of your effort."*

We can use mindfulness to attack pessimism. Mindfulness is about non-judgmentally accepting the present moment and choosing where you will put your full attention. We can use mindfulness to:

1. Acknowledge the mixed messages (and/or cognitive distortions) that you hear internally.

2. Choose to turn down the volume on the negative messages. Visualize turning the volume knob down. This involves that you CHOOSE to stop clinging to the negative statements. Stop yourself from looking for reasons the thoughts are right, stop twisting reality. Imagine dropping the thoughts on the ground and walking away.

3. Now choose to turn your attention TOWARD the volume knob on

the healthier thoughts and turn the volume up! These thoughts may not be overtly positive; they may be neutral, and that is ok. They could maybe be thoughts instead of absolutes (i.e., *"Maybe I will have a decent day," "Maybe I will enjoy the get together," "Maybe today will be better than I think," "Perhaps I will be able to learn new ways to interact with money"*). The thoughts COULD even be positive! (Ex. *"I am excited to stick to this budget," "I am proud of myself for _____," "I know my family loves me"*).

I am NOT suggesting that you go from Debbie Downer to Suzy Sunshine all at once. Normal Nancy is a great gal! Come visit me in the land of average and see if you can turn away from pessimistic, negative, all-or-nothing thinking and turn toward neutral, content, average thinking. Bonus points for allowing yourself to think 1-2 optimistic thoughts each day!

Skills: Check the Facts and Mindfulness of Our Thoughts

If you would consider yourself a pessimist, well done! You successfully use four major thinking errors with regularity! That is quite an accomplishment. Please note my sarcasm –this is a huge problem. If one is stuck in pessimistic thoughts related to their finances, it can be a downward spiral of shame, anger, and hopelessness that is difficult to turn around. The practical idea presented here as a treatment for pessimistic thinking habits is to talk back! What I mean is that you need to begin talking back to those thoughts (just as you would to another person who was speaking abusively to you)! The first skill we need to tap into here, again, is mindfulness. With mindful awareness, I need you to notice where your thinking errors are occurring. As you read the previous pages, did you notice any similar habits that you might have? Once you identify the problematic thought, it is crucial to name it and tame it. In DBT® we do this using the Check the Facts skill. Checking the facts allows us to recognize that our belief/interpretation of an event dictates what sorts of body sensations, urges, and actions we take. To check the facts, one must:

1. Identify what belief you have about your financial behaviors. (Ex. *I am an idiot for not checking my balance. Now I have late fees that I can't afford.*)

2. Notice what urges and bodily sensations you have as a result of your interpretation. (Ex. *I want to go shopping because I am already so far in debt, who cares? I feel heavy, empty, and alone. I want to hide.*)

3. Become aware of how you are increasing your own suffering and how a different style of self-talk might decrease your

suffering. Rather than being overly positive about your mistake, work to simply describe the situation, as well as your feelings and consequences. (Ex. I avoided checking my balance for one week, which led to me over-drawing and now I have added fees. I am disappointed in my choice, and I need to come up with a different plan for next month.)

4. Praise yourself for thinking differently. (Ex. *I believe that I can decrease my shame with healthier self-talk, which will help me gain control of my self-sabotaging behaviors! I am proud of how hard I am trying.*)

To take check the facts one step further, it is also helpful to validate your own fears and come up with a plan for if the "worst case scenario" really does come true. To do this, you ask yourself the following questions:

1. What am I afraid will happen?
Ex. *I am afraid that if I check my balance regularly, I will have to figure out how to cope with the shame that I spend more than I bring in.*

2. What is the associated catastrophe?
Ex. *I will realize that I need to file for bankruptcy or that I need to get a second job.*

3. How can I cope if that becomes a reality?
Ex. *As I do not understand bankruptcy law, I would consult with a specialized attorney to get coaching. If I needed to get a second job, I could use positive self-talk to remind myself that it is only for a short time. I could also work on finding a work-from-home type position or ask my current employer for additional responsibilities. In a pinch, I could always babysit or offer to clean people's homes, as these are two of my strengths.*

As bizarre as it may seem, you do have the ability to control your thoughts! By and large, this seems to be a difficult concept for most people to grasp ...like a mystic urban legend. I'm here to talk to you about exactly how it's done! As previously discussed, mindfulness is all about noticing and being aware of what is happening in and around you while remaining compassionate and non-judgmental. So how does this relate to thoughts you ask? First things first:
1. You must become aware of your thoughts: their patterns, intensity, nature, etc.
2. Take a step back and just pause. Breathe. Your breath is ALWAYS there for you; use it as your anchor.
3. Observe any urges associated with your thoughts. Do you have an urge

to minimize it, block it, or suppress it? Do you have an urge to maximize it, exaggerate it, or cling to it? Neither of these options is mindfully allowing the thought to pass. Just as you would a raccoon on a trail hike, just notice the thought, acknowledge it, and keep on walking. No need to taunt it, no need to kick it, no need to feed it, either!

4. Make a choice to mindfully (with intention) re-enter your day. Make a choice to be effective in the scenario you are in. This may mean problem solving, it may mean having a difficult conversation, it may mean LETTING GO of nagging thoughts.

You have so many options with thoughts, it's a shame to just give into every single one and be at their mercy. Just because you have a thought, does not mean you need to act on it (let's face it ...that could be awkward in some situations!). Just because you have a thought does not make it a FACT. (Come on ...did any of us see Pluto getting his planet status revoked!). Just because a thought is intense or pervasive does not mean it's more important than other less frequent thoughts. I urge you to take some time and consider these concepts. You may not have the ability to control which thoughts pop into your head ...you DO have the ability to control what you do with them, though!

Skill Practice: Check the Facts

To create a healthier interpretation for yourself, thus reducing your problematic urges and behaviors, you need to jot down what pessimistic thoughts you are having about your financial behaviors. After each statement, note what emotion you feel when thinking the statement:

Ex. *I will never have a cushion of emergency money in my savings account because I have no self-control (shame).*

1. _____

2. _____

3. _____

4. _____

5. _____

Next, please jot down a rational minded challenge statement for each pessimistic thought. This rational challenge needs to be free of judgments about yourself or the situation. Notice the lack of negative emotions when you think each of the challenges:

Ex: *I struggle with impulsive purchases, which has led to me using savings. I will work on coping with my urges so that I can build up my savings account for emergencies.*

1. _____

2. _____

3. _____

4. _____

5. _____

Skill Practice: Check the Facts (cont.)

Lastly in check the facts, we do need to validate ourselves and our fears. Ask yourself and write the answers below:

1. What am I afraid will happen?

2. What is the associated catastrophe?

3. How can I cope if that becomes a reality?

Makin' Bacon as Opposite Action

The last topic related to money addresses the fear that many people have about their own personal capacity for work. Many people in my personal circle and that I encounter professionally have either been told that they *shouldn't work* or that they *can't handle* work. Many people have had bad experiences with prior employers or in emotional flare-ups that have led them to believe that they are *not capable* of coping.

I want you to know that you CAN cope, you ARE capable, and you can use gainful employment as a means toward gaining purpose and self-worth. It is true that your symptoms of depression, anxiety or anger can flare-up from time to time which may result in difficult seasons related to employment; however, giving in and ceasing work often leads to bigger spirals and worsening symptoms. Purpose in your day/schedule is essential for identity and self-worth.

Your thoughts, emotions and behaviors are all connected and feed into each other (for better or for worse).

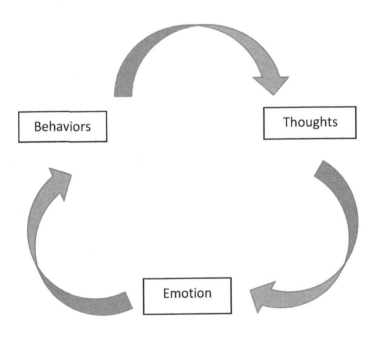

Consider this example related to employment:

Thought: *I am so overwhelmed with the fight I just had with my mom; I could never get through a day at work.*
Behavior: *Call off work*
Emotion: *Guilt*
Thought: *I know my co-workers are going to be angry at me for leaving them in a pinch*
Behavior: *Post to social media about how "sick" I am*
Emotion: *Shame*
Thought: *I am so pathetic, now I won't even have enough money to cover rent this week*
Behavior: *Ruminate on all my mistakes in recent months*
Emotion: *Self-hatred, sadness*
Thought: *Why do I even try? I screw everything up.*
Behavior: *Lie in bed all day, overeat*
Emotion: *Depression*

Work, in and of itself, can be a form of the skill opposite action. It is crucial that you keep your commitments at work, if possible, as it can propel you forward and keep you from spiraling downward. You will get more out of it if you also work to have opposite thoughts, body language, and physiology. Even your hygiene will play a role.

Take the same example with a skillful twist:

Thought: *I am so overwhelmed with the fight I just had with my mom; I could never get through a day at work.*
Behavior: *Listen to uplifting music while driving to work*
Emotion: *Sad about fight, proud of choice to go to work*
Thought: *I know my co-workers are going to be glad that I came in and didn't leaving them in a pinch*
Behavior: *Half-smile and walk with confident posture*
Emotion: *Content*
Thought: *I am so proud of myself. I didn't think I could do this, and I am actually doing fairly well!*
Behavior: *Reward self with a coffee with co-workers after shift*
Emotion: *Enjoyment*
Thought: *I do have the energy to call mom back and apologize for my side of things*
Behavior: *Call mom, apologize, make plans for lunch this weekend*
Emotion: *relief*

Taking it a step further we could examine how energized and confident we may feel in that same example if dressed nicely. You would never wear sweatpants or pajamas on a first date (I hope)! You would not go to a job interview with your hair a mess and not showering for three days (I hope!). One function of your attire is to communicate to others who you are and how you want to be treated. Pajamas in public do not communicate a desire for respect. Your attire also communicates to YOURSELF! I know that when I am dressed nicely, my posture is better, my confidence is up, my eye contact is improved; low and behold, I am in a better mood! If we added this after the first thought:

Behavior: *bathe, use products (lotion, hair products, perfume/cologne) and wear the nicest clothes that are socially appropriate for your daily tasks*
We might also find a side effect of:
Emotion: *Pride*
Behavior: *Tall posture, smiling*
Thought: *"I've got this!"*

I PROMISE that it will ease up your undesired mood. These actions do not fix depression —they are not a replacement for medication and/or therapy; however, they are an excellent and inexpensive step toward you regaining control.

Thoughts, feelings, behaviors. They are all connected; and the relationship is transactional. This means that while one influences another, that change will in turn influence another factor. None of the three can exist without the other two. This begs the question —where do we make the change in our lives if we have suffering? Do you change what thoughts you have; do you change your actions before or after the thoughts, or do you change how you feel about the situation? The answer is ANY of the three will elicit change; however, as Jerry Sternin said, "It's easier to act your way into a new way of thinking, than think your way into a new way of acting.". Feelings will happen afterward and will be in alignment with your actions and/or your thoughts.

We know it is one of the HARDEST things to do, to act differently than we may feel. Think back to the last time you were feeling depressed; I bet it would have been really hard to get you to go exercise! The last time you were really anxious, I bet it would have been hard to convince you to go lie down and listen to a meditation. And the last time you were fuming mad, I bet it would have been difficult to get you to go for a walk ...and yet this is what I suggest! Why would I suggest something so radically difficult? Mainly because if you do, you will see how quickly it remedies the intensity of the emotion and thoughts. I propose that if you do it a few times in a row, you will begin to trust the process; this is pretty much what all people with good habits say about how they stick to their routines! So, work on doing the opposite of your (ineffective) urge and see if the thoughts and feelings come along in a helpful way!

Work is the crux here, the key to change. Without a distraction, we often fall into the pit of despair. We all need a purpose. As you age and move through life, I also hope that your jobs become more and more in line with your values as well. While the menial labor of adolescence and early adulthood serve an important role in our society, they often do not give a person's life meaning and direction. I hope for you that as you watch your employment history unfold, each step helps you reach the goal of a "wise-minded" job fit, one that makes you feel like you are living aligned with your values.

Reflect by journaling: Employment

Take some time to reflect on how taking action toward life purpose can help keep you out of a downward emotional spiral. Also reflect on whether your current type of employment/volunteering/schooling (or lack thereof) is serving a healthy role in your self-esteem. If not, how can you work toward a healthier job fit?

6 IT RUNS IN THE FAMILY

When we ask someone to tell us about their family, it us usually an emotionally charged answer we receive. What I introduce in this chapter can help, whether you feel positively, negatively, or neutrally about your upbringing and whether you feel positively, negatively, or neutrally about your current family functioning. Learning to apply these ideas will most certainly help you in your future family endeavors and will most certainly help you become less reactive in other realms as well!

What I see with people who are dissatisfied with their family situations (regardless of who is "at fault") is a higher tendency toward: judgments (which includes shoulds and assumptions) and expectations. We will break each of these down and teach skillful means for each pitfall below.

Skill: Non-Judgmental

In short, judgments are when you decide that your interpretation is a fact and assume that everyone would agree. When you judge, you are placing your own perceptions high above everyone else's. Judgment can be either positive (ex: "*Oh my gosh, that is SO AWESOME!!!*" or "*You look great today!*") or they can be negative (ex. "*I can't even stand it; it's terrible!*" or "*My dad it such a jerk!*"). Whether positive or negative, judgments have the following in common: it is a fickle habit and judgments do not give us much information to work with. Fickle means that something is likely to change easily; a person who is quick to say something is "*awesome,*" "*amazing,*" or "*fun*" is just as likely to say things are "*awful,*" "*sucky,*" or "*terrible.*" This will result in people not seeing you as a reliable source. In line with this, I want you to understand that if you are a frequent user of the types of words, your word does not mean as much to others, as they know it is a superficial judgment and you are likely to change your mind.

Within the context of DBT®, we try very hard to remove judgments and replace them with a non-judgmental description. When this happens, an "awesome ride" becomes "a roller coaster with 6 inversions that caused you to feel excited" or having a dad that's a "jerk" becomes "disappointment that my dad forgot to call me back." When you put a judgmental label on someone without context, people don't know what to do to be helpful. They do not have enough information to respond effectively. A reduction in judgments will result in your needs getting met more efficiently, people wanting to spend more time around you, and a healthier worldview overall. When people view you as a negative complainer, they may start to avoid you. If people view you as a person who speaks their truth about what happened, you may be seen as more reliable. By describing the facts instead of judging, you can teach yourself to advocate for your needs in a way that others will respect and listen. This is a LOADED skill here …do not read on until you have fully absorbed the last paragraph.

Furthermore, we can only describe things that we actually observed. In short, this means that you cannot know what a person's intentions, feelings, thoughts, assumptions, judgments, etc. were. You can only observe their body language, words, tone, etc. By sticking to what you can observe, you will reduce the amount of drama and gossip in your life!

"Shoulds" as a Type of Judgment

When you "should" on someone else, you are judging them. Using the word "should" toward someone else's behavior indicates that you know what is best for them. "Shoulding" on other people almost always leads to anger, either in the form of annoyance, irritability, or direct anger at another person. Paradoxically, when you "should" on yourself, you are judging yourself. Using it towards yourself is like putting yourself down or calling yourself stupid. "Shoulding" on yourself almost always leads to shame. Most people have a desire to feel less anger and less shame; simply rephrasing your "shoulds" can have that effect! This relates especially strongly within families because anger and shame in families can cause deep rifts, avoidance between family members, and an increase in lying to one another.

Dictionary.com defines should as:
   verb
   1. used to indicate obligation, duty, or correctness, typically when criticizing someone's actions.

   Even the dictionary knows you are using the word should to judge people!
   To combat the "should", I recommend that people replace the "should" with a curious wondering. For example: "*You should have been here by 9*" could be rephrased as "*I wonder if you would have been less stressed if you arrived*

earlier?" You can always add your feeling or thought, if they are appropriately labeled: "*I noticed that I felt worried as I had the thought that you may have been in an accident.*" It may seem tedious to label your thoughts as thoughts and your feelings as feelings; however, it will save you from being misunderstood and that will save you a lot of time down the road from arguing and being in conflict! I have noticed that people do not like when another person insinuates that they have poor decision-making skills; therefore, the second "wondering with" strategy is likely to feel less threatening. The strategy of "wondering with" a person can be applied across the board to reduce interpersonal conflict. Joining others where they are (aka treating yourself as though you are of equal worth and intelligence) will allow your ideas to be much more well-received. No one likes a smart-alek or know-it-all.

Another way people run into problems with "shoulding" as it relates to family dynamics is by "shoulding" on themselves. This takes on the opposite role of "shoulding" on others. When you "should" on yourself, I believe it is in indication of low self-esteem. "*I should have known that would have hurt my mom's feelings*" indicates that you are ignorant in some way for not having been able to see into the future. You can reframe the "self-shoulding" statement by stating what you are experiencing: "*I am feeling guilt for hurting my mom's feelings.*" You can also add in your desires or a change you plan to make: "*I would like the chance to apologize, and in the future, I will be more mindful of how my words affect others.*"

Assumptions as Judgments

An assumption is a belief that you hold to be factually true, without any proof. Assumptions also tend to follow you thinking that you know better/more than others. In families, there are often generations-old assumptions about other types of people, sects of the family, younger generations vs older generations, etc., which can be difficult to break! Assumptions inevitably pave the way for judgments to occur; unfortunately, this can prohibit future generations to experience each other!

My suggestion for assumptions is to notice when they are occurring or where in your family they tend to live. Once you have captured the assumption, you can then begin the tedious task of re-wording it into a more descriptive statement. Instead of saying, "*Mom hates Aunt Sue, and inviting both of them would be a disaster,*" you could say "*Mom was annoyed with Aunt Sue's comments about her pie last Thanksgiving; perhaps this year they will get along better because I will bake the pies!*" One can also just point out the assumption on their path toward becoming less judgmental: "*I am noticing that I tend to assume that Uncle Lou will offend me before I even see him.*" Noticing a thought as just a thought can open some space for another truth to grow.

In lieu of judging or assuming, a safe alternative is always to state the fact and your feeling. When I am not sure how to say something, I try to stick with what I factually observed and what my resulting emotion was. This is not generally something anyone can argue with. Instead of saying *"Math is stupid,"* I could more skillfully say, *"When I try math, I often make errors, which makes me feel incompetent."* This can be applied in family situations just as well. Instead of saying, *"My brother is so disrespectful,"* I could say, *"My brother did not call me on my birthday, and I felt sad about this."* People generally respond better to this second type of statement (the fact and the feeling).

Skill Practice: Overcoming Judgments

Make a list of five judgments (of others) that you make often, then rephrase it to be a non-judgmental description. You can always include the emotion you feel or potential consequences if you feel that is helpful to the situation. These can include "shoulds" or be any type of judgmental statement.

Example: *My brother does not care about anyone but himself. He is selfish.*

Rephrased: I *felt angry when my brother insisted, we meet at his house because it's not*

convenient for me. I noticed that I thought he was selfish.

1._____

_____

_____

2._____

_____

_____

3._____

_____

_____

4._____

_____

_____

5._____

_____

_____

Now try to do the same of self-judgments. These can include "should" or be flat out judgmental thoughts you have about yourself.

Example: *I am annoying. My family does not like to be around me.* (*Note that this example is a judgment followed by an assumption*) Reframe: *I worry that I annoy my family, as they cancelled our plans. I had the thought that they do not want to spend time with me, which makes me sad.*

1._____

_____

_____

2._____

_____

_____

3._____

_____

_____

4._____

_____

_____

5._____

_____

_____

Lastly, think of an assumption that you have about a family member and try to be more descriptive.

Example: *My in-laws are always late because they don't like me can be reframed as I notice the thought that my in-laws do not like me because they tend to be late.*

Assumption:

_____

_____

Reframe:

_____

_____

Your Backpack of Resentment

Another cognitive pitfall we tend to have with our families that impedes progress is the habit of carrying around a backpack full of rocks. This is, of course, an analogy: the rocks are the resentment and hurt feelings you have experienced over your lifetime, and the backpack is your refusal to accept that we cannot change the past. I have noticed that people have the belief that there is some sort of magic apology or gesture that will alleviate the pain; however, the truth is that only your forgiveness of that person and their actions (paired with radical acceptance) can alleviate the pain.

Radical acceptance is a heavy skill. Once explained, most people have an initial reaction of anger. I am asking that you keep an open mind about this idea. Radical comes from the Latin word for root, and what I am encouraging you to do is to work on this skill to your core (your root). Acceptance does not equate to approval, enjoyment, or love of the situation. Acceptance does not mean that you hope it will happen again or that you are going to be a doormat in the future. Acceptance means that you acknowledge that an event has occurred (or is occurring). That's it. You acknowledge that an event has occurred (or is occurring) AND you are choosing the path of less suffering by choosing to stop throwing temper tantrums, ruminating, or acting in ways that keep you fuming. Acceptance allows you to put down all the bitterness, the hate, the anger ...and live your life according to your values. Look at the illustration here to work on comprehending how we can free ourselves from those negative emotions:

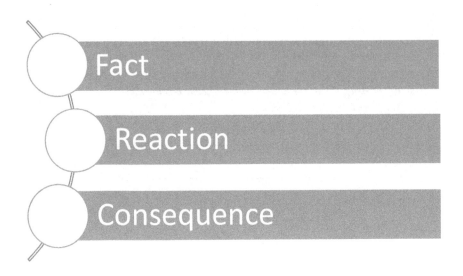

Fact: The fact is what you have experienced or are experiencing. Example: *My sister stole from me*

Reaction: The reaction is what you do as a result. *I do not speak to her or my nieces for 2 years.*

Consequence: The consequence is what results from your reaction. *I feel anger and hatred. I am not invited to my niece's school plays or birthday dinners. I feel abandoned by my family. I have a damaged relationship with all involved.*

Notice I said reaction and not response. I intend to teach you how a different response will lead to less suffering in the consequences. In no way am I suggesting that you love your sister's theft behavior, nor am I suggesting that you allow her to keep stealing from you. Depending on the situation, a healthy reaction may include less contact, no contact, or no change. To figure all this out, you must first evaluate what your long-term goal is. For this example, let's say your long-term goal is to stay in your niece's lives and continue to be involved with your core family. You want to have healthier boundaries with your sister. In that case, you need a different reaction to help you achieve your long-term goals. Other possible reactions you could choose (not an exhaustive list) are:

1. Remain in contact on social media for several months; slowly begin to spend time with them at neutral locations.

2. Not only cut them out of your life —regularly insult her in texts and on social media as well.

3. Allow your sister and her daughters to move in with you.

4. Ask your sister to go to dinner with you and explain your feelings; ask her how she thinks the two of you can work together to move forward and build trust.

5. Make no changes. Act like nothing happened.

Take a moment to consider what the correlated consequences would be with each chosen response. Which do you think makes the most sense (considering your long-term goals)? Can you think of other effective solutions? Radical acceptance as a skill encourages you to recognize the fact portion of your various scenarios. The skill does not encourage you to love the fact; however, one must accept that the fact is indeed a reality in order to stop making it worse! The applications are endless: gas prices jumping on the day your gas light comes on, a particular family member's personality, diagnoses of you or your loved one(s), politics ...all these things exist and cannot be immediately changed. Our expectations, wishes, and demands cause us to react unskillfully and have increased suffering with our consequences. Radical acceptance provides a fantastic kind of freedom! When you learn that you do not HAVE to be angry about the happenings in life, you learn that you are in control of your moods, attitudes, and suffering.

Skill Practice: Radical Acceptance

Fill in the charts below with several non-triggering life facts/things that are going to happen whether you want them to or not (i.e., bills, flu shot, family traditions, speed limits). Under the reaction section, identify what you typically do in response. Then note what consequences (good, bad, or otherwise) that you experience. Evaluate whether your response and your consequence will help you meet your long-term goals or not. If not, this is an indication that you may need to try a different response to garner a different reaction.

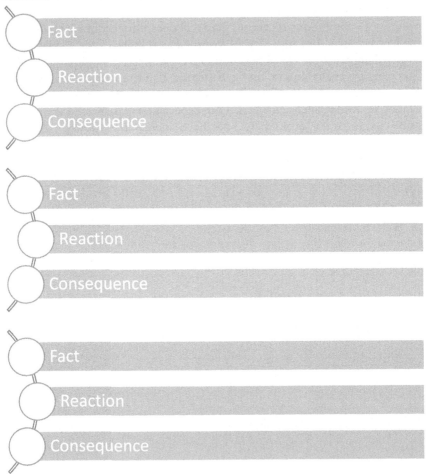

As you develop this skill, you can work on more difficult facts. Feel free to copy these pages as many times as possible to hone the skill.

Expectations

The last significant problem that we tend to find related to problems we have within our families is having expectations. Having expectations of other people leads to anxiety, disappointment, and resentment. Expectations also insinuate that you want people to act according to your standards and that your standards are "right," whereas the family members are "wrong."

Your expectations of others can lead to anxiety because what you think should happen may or may not. As a result, you feel anxious about the impending disappointment. This can sabotage the whole interaction as you are not actually present while interacting with the other person! The strategy to cure this ailment is to be a mindful communicator. Mindful interactions require you to fully engage while turning your internal mental chatter off. Mindful communication means that you put your phone down, make eye contact, and listen to what the other person is saying. Unfortunately, we often listen only so that we can attack back, without fully hearing what the other person is saying.

Your expectations of others also leads to disappointment because it is not possible to predict another human's behaviors with 100% accuracy. When you walk into an interaction with your own pre-planned agenda, you are ensuring disappointment. Disappointment can grow and lead to anger and resentment …none of those emotions are pleasant!

My recommendation is that you enter into family interactions with curiosity. Curiosity allows for the interaction to unfold holistically, the likelihood of arguments plummets. If you have a request of a person, consider wondering with them rather than demanding. This would look like you saying, "*I wonder if we can work together on Thanksgiving dinner this year*" instead of saying "*You need to make the sides and I will make the turkey.*" No one likes to be told what to do….

Reflection by Journaling: Do you tend to have high expectations of others in your family? Does that turn out well for you? Who can you identify to practice reducing expectations? What do you think about being more mindful and curious in your interactions? What do you think about "wondering with" as a strategy to reduce conflict?

How-To Communicate

The background ideas I have presented thus far are all well and good; however, the question still lingers: *"How do I communicate more efficiently?"* I have a tried-and-true DBT® communication equation for you: DEARMAN. DEARMAN is an acronym that reminds you what components need to be included when you communicate. DEARMAN increases the likelihood that you will maintain your integrity and be heard, whether or not the person does what you want. Historically, many of us fixate on the demand, while forgetting to tell people why the heck they should care! Think about how you feel when people bark an order at you (*"Clean your room!" "I need you to stay late tonight."* or *"Show up at 10"*) without telling you why, it goes over like a lead balloon! Explore the equation below:

D – Describe: state the facts of what the situation is. Do not assume the other person knows what you're referring to. Do not include embellishments or judgments. (*I   noticed   that*_____, or *When* _____*happened*)

E – Express: tell them how you feel and/or what your opinions are! Do not   assume   others   can   read   your   mind!   (*I   feel* _____)

A – Assert/Ask: state what the request is. Be clear and keep your tone neutral. Wondering with is a good strategy here. (*I would like*_____, *Could you* _____, *I'm wondering if*_____)

R – Reinforce: Tell them why they will benefit from doing what you are asking of them. This is not meaning to threaten – rather, to state out the positive consequences of their compliance. (*so that*_____)

Examples of DEARMAN:

1. *I noticed your floor is looking cluttered, and I am afraid you will step on something in the middle of the night. Could you get the laundry up off the floor so that you aren't as likely to get hurt?*

2. *I just found out that we missed a deadline as an agency. I was told that if we can get the report turned in by 8pm, it will be accepted. Could you please stay late tonight, and you will be compensated time-and-a-half?*

3. *I am feeling anxious about our road trip tomorrow. Could you try and meet me at 10 AM so that we are less pressed for time?*

The DEAR portion of the DEARMAN strategy really gets your authentic, thought-out point across and increases the likelihood that you do so in a respectable manner. Before we look at the rest of the strategy associated with DEARMAN, take time to practice! Take some time to write a few scripts in your journal.

The MAN part of DEARMAN alludes to the fact that there are three things a person needs to consider when they are asking someone for something (this can also be used to decline someone else's request or to structure a difficult talk). Each objective has an associated acronym that addresses exactly how to deliver the DEAR sentence(s).

1. Consider your objective. What do you want? What are you trying to achieve? The MAN acronym below will allow you to work on this.

2. Consider your relationship. How do you want the other person to feel about you AFTER the interaction? Remember the theme here –we are working on long-term goals, not short-term urges. Attacking the person verbally might feel good short-term yet is unlikely to help you achieve long-term goals. The GIVE acronym will allow you to preserve the relationship.

3. Consider self-respect. How do you want to feel about yourself after the interaction? The FAST acronym will encourage you to preserve your own values and self-respect.

Most interactions require a smattering of the three objectives. It is similar to a recipe; however, it is imperative that you decide which is first, second, and third. If someone asks you to do something that is against your values, you may find that you need a heaping serving of self-respect (FAST), a scoop of your objective (MAN) and that the relationship isn't particularly important at all. That combination would allow you to say "no" in a way that you are proud of!

When your objective is number one, the strategy you will use the most of is MAN. MAN is an acronym standing for:

M – Stay Mindful: Keep the focus on the topic at hand. Resist the urge to "beat around the bush" or to let yourself get distracted by attempts to derail the conversation.

A – Appear Confident: This is especially difficult when you are anxious or feel shame. Have good eye contact and confident body posture!

N – Negotiate: Remember that you often need to give to get. You may need to accept less than you are comfortable with if the long-term goal is being achieved.

When the relationship is number one (it often is with family situations), the strategy you will use the most of is called "GIVE". GIVE is an acronym standing for:

G – Be Gentle: This means be gentle with yourself and the other person.

I – Act Interested: Yes. ACT! If the relationship is important, hear them out or express interest in their needs/wants. You don't have to change your stance but hearing them out will protect the relationship.

V – Validate: Validating means that you find the grain of truth about what the other person is saying and say it out loud! This often includes acknowledging their feelings/interpretations. Examples include: "*I can see why…*" "*I can see how passionate you feel about this,* or "*I think I would feel that way too!"*

E – Use an Easy Manner: Be authentically yourself, which may include a sense of humor. Soften up what you say and how you say it.

When the number one objective is self-respect, the strategy is FAST. FAST is an acronym that stands for:

F – Be Fair: Be fair to your needs and the other person's needs.

A – No Apologies: Do not be overly apologetic! We all tend to overuse *"I'm sorry"* as a sentence starter. I suggest you use DEAR and then add a *"thank you"* when they answer. (If they say no, you could say, *"Thank you for considering/ taking time to hear me out"*).

S – Stick to Your Values: This requires you to evaluate your values and know what they are! Don't do things that make you feel immoral. You can even say *"I value honesty, so..."* or *"I value hard work, which is why this is important to me."*

T – Be Truthful: Tell the truth; do not act helpless or manipulative.

Once you evaluate your scenario, applying the MAN, GIVE, or FAST strategies is like driving and determining how much to push on the gas, brake, and clutch. Sometimes it will be 90% MAN, 5% GIVE, and 5% FAST (such as interacting with a used car salesman you are unlikely to see again), sometimes it will be 20% MAN, 60% GIVE, and 20% FAST (such as asking your grandma to make a pie for you) or you may see a situation that is 10% MAN, 10% GIVE, and 80% FAST (such as asking your sibling to not drink around you due to recent sobriety). The rankings could be different for three different people in the same scenario; you must evaluate your situation in wise mind.

Skill Practice: DEARMAN

What is the situation?

What is the objective?   Relationship goal?   Self-respect goal?

Take time to write out your script (as if you would be reading it to the other person):

Self-care

An under-utilized topic that I deem necessary to this chapter is the need for self-care. When tension is high, we are less likely to be skillful or eloquent with our words. If you find yourself feeling stressed-out over family functions, I encourage you to schedule some wise-minded time before AND after the family gathering. Time prior to the engagement can help you get into a healthier mindset by reminding yourself to use the strategies in this chapter. Working to lower your expectations, using positive self-talk, being empathetic and validating towards yourself as well as your family members will go a long way to improve your experience of family dynamics. After the family interaction, this time can help you decompress and have gentle internal dialogue with less self-sabotage and resulting shame.

To prepare yourself for optimal mental health during family functions, I highly suggest you bring self-care items with you. Discreet items such as lip balm, lotion, photos on your phone, downloaded self-care/mental health apps, your favorite soothing beverage, and hard candy are easiest to benefit from. There is research behind lavender as a scent and peppermint as a taste that are especially helpful for stress (Koulivand et al, 2013; Perry and Perry, 2006).

Refresher on Willingness:

As discussed in previous chapters, a necessary tool for you to keep in mind with family dynamics is to be WILLING. Willingness means that you are going to do what is necessary/effective regardless of whether you want to. Willingness is when you stop fighting reality and allow the ways of the world to be just as they are, instead of how you want them to be (including family dynamics as long as they are not abusive). Willingness is likened to playing the hand you were dealt instead of the hand you wish you were dealt. Willingness is living by the paycheck you have, not the one you wish you had! Willingness is the opposite of stubborn. Families tend to have a lot of stubborn, long held beliefs that are no longer healthy or helpful. Be the one that is willing to let the pot settle (rather than stirring the pot)! This means you must be willing to use the strategies discussed in this chapter if you want your family dynamics to change, even if you are not the one who "started it."

Reflect by Journaling: In what ways do you think you could improve self-care surrounding family affairs? In what ways are you willing to admit that you are a bit stubborn? Can you work on being more willing within your family relationships?

7 FRIENDSHIP GARDEN

Where We Go Wrong

Overall, I notice several primary factors that impede having a healthy and fulfilling social life, and each will be addressed in this chapter. Social anxiety, myths/faulty assumptions, avoidance, and stress are among them most frequent barriers. It is important to explore what might be hindering your social connectivity prior to problem solving; if not, we tend to apply strategies that won't solve the right problem!

Social anxiety is quite possibly the biggest umbrella excuse for why people don't go places to meet and connect with other people. Social anxiety exists on a spectrum from self-doubt to full on agoraphobia and/or panic disorder. Anxiety is a difficult beast to conquer, regardless of its form because anxiety attacks at a primal level. When a person feels anxiety, their brain secretes cortisol and adrenaline (among other things), which leads to a fight, flight, or freeze reaction. If this has ever happened to you, you know how unhelpful suggestions to "just breathe" or "just go" to an event can be. If we are going to attack social anxiety at its core, we must fight fire with fire. Cheerleading yourself out of anxiety is about as helpful as an umbrella in a hurricane. The DBT® skills that I suggest you employ are half-smile and willing hands. There is new research emerging on other body language life-hacks such as power posing and eyebrow raising. I am aware of how ridiculous this sounds to a first-time reader. When I first learned the skill of half-smiling, I thought there was no way I could teach it! No one would take me seriously! As any good therapist would do, I had to practice it (a lot) prior to teaching it. I needed anecdotal evidence that it would work to pair with the scientific research.

The way that I practiced half-smiling was to make an inner commitment to half-smile each time I saw my street sign and hold the expression until I got into my house. The results were astounding! The mood shift that happened from half-smiling for two minutes was life-changing!

Skill: Half-Smile

To half-smile, you need to let go of any judgments you have about the name. It is a poorly named skill in my opinion. It is not about a fake smile or a Cheshire-cat-meets-Joker-from-Batman evil grin; rather, it is about putting a pleasant expression on your face. Paul Ekman has found in his research on micro-expressions that "feel good" chemicals are released in the brain whenever the smile contains the "ducane marker" (which is similar to crow's feet). Those who have watched America's Next Top Model will be familiar with host Tyra Bank's instructing the participants to smize (smile with your eyes). A half- smile really is not very noticeable to anyone that might see you, it is more of an internal experience of a pleased expression which might show on your face with ever-so-slightly upturned corners of your mouth and barely visible crow's feet tugging at your temples. One might look at you and wonder what you are thinking about, as if you just recalled a happy memory.

The power-couple spouse of the half-smile (think Jay-Z and Bey) is to utilize willing hands. Willing hands is an action skill. You must unclench your fists and open your hands, palm up. This can be done in any posture (sitting, standing, or lying down) and, again, isn't very noticeable to others. Open palms are a universal gesture of peace and safety. Think about it: if you were in danger, you would not have a pleasant expression or open hands, you would adopt a firm face and muscle tension that can allow you to act (fight or flee) if necessary. I have had countless clients tell me how, after learning this skill, they noticed how they even sleep with their hands in a fist! Releasing the fists and sleeping with open palms (under your pillow even) has shown reduced anxiety, nightmares, and insomnia!

Adjunct with half-smile and willing hands are power poses, eyebrow raises and siting on the floor. All the suggested body language alterations have an impact on actual measurable brain chemistry. Power posing is an idea being researched heavily by Ann Cuddy. She has found that two minutes of standing confidently (yes, think superman) has an immediate reaction in the brain in the form of reduced cortisol. She suggests that before entering a situation that makes you feel anxious (if the anxiety is unproductive), you should go into a private space and stand confidently for two minutes. Conversely, anxiety poses (touching neck, turning inward, avoiding eye contact, slouching) have the immediate result of raising cortisol and decreasing testosterone, which leaves you feeling anxious and powerless! When you notice yourself doing this (playing with a necklace, resting your hand on your neck/chest, walking with head down and/or hands in pocket, it is crucial that you immediately undo the anxiety pose and add in whatever degree of half-smile, willing hands, or power posing is socially acceptable. Eyebrow raises are a universal expression of welcoming, which only happens when a person experiences safety. Raising your eyebrows and leaning in communicates a willingness to learn more and connect with someone; the side effect of this is genuine connection. It is found to be effective for a person to practice raising their eyebrows prior to entering the social situation. I personally notice a natural half smile occurs with this practice, which is a win-win. Lastly, I will present some research that I learned about from a dietician. When a person experiences stomach-upset after eating, dieticians have found that it is often stress-related (as found with IBS symptoms). If you are anxious, and you eat, the food is not actually digested/absorbed effectively because of the evolutionary link to cortisol. Anxiety produces cortisol, and cortisol makes you think your life is in jeopardy. If you take a zebra, for example, and measure its cortisol before and after being chased by a predator, you will find that cortisol spikes when the chase is happening. The spike of cortisol shuts down the body's digestion, reproductive system, immune system, etc., to channel ALL of the animal's energy into increased heart rate and blood flow to the muscles to allow it to run away and escape! This is a cool trick our body does, except that we aren't in danger as often as our body perceives we are. When you have chronic stress, your body does not have healthy digestive processes, often times menstrual cycles are disrupted, and/or the person gets sick a lot due to immunity disruptions. This is, again, not a place that we can cheerlead ourselves out of; however, we can outsmart our body by sitting on the floor. You would NEVER sit on the floor if you were in danger; therefore, the act of sitting on the floor tells your brain that you are safe and allows the cortisol to stop being secreted. This short-circuits your anxiety and calms you down! Ever notice how much calmer you are after playing with a young child on the floor? If possible, in social settings that make you nervous: have a calm/pleasant facial expression, sit down with open posture (do not cross arms or legs), lean in and raise eyebrows while listening, and sit low to the ground if possible. This combination leaves social anxiety incapable of taking over.

Skill: Myths

Myths are another problem that impede our social lives. A myth is a statement that we believe to be true, despite not having any facts to support it. A myth is often all-or-nothing in nature and is a belief that we have been telling ourselves over the years (*I don't like people,* etc.) Myths can stop progress before it even has a chance to start. The trick with a myth is to notice it or be open to another person pointing it out and then reframe it in a less absolute, dare I say, more dialectical frame.

Here are some examples of myths related to social connectedness:

1. I don't need friends.
2. People don't like me.
3. If I talk to someone new, they will reject me.

4. I can't handle people being mad at me.

5. I am a loser and that's why no one invites me to do anything.

6. I don't care.

7. No one likes the same things I do, it's better to stay isolated.

To challenge a myth, you must recognize how black-and-white it is and work in the grey, so to speak. Below, I will write a challenge to the seven myths above:

1. I feel anxiety about being rejected, and I am aware that social connection is something I desire deeply.

2. While it may be true that some people do not care for my personality/interest, it is not true that all people will hate me. I can keep working to find the right fit.

3. I have no way to predict the future, and I have skills to increase the likelihood of both connecting successfully and tolerating discomfort of failed attempts.

4. I am learning ways to cope with uncomfortable feelings.

5. It is possible that people do not call me because they don't want to bother me or because I have acted unfriendly and therefore, they don't think I'd want to come.

6. I do care; me pushing people away is an attempt to keep myself safe.

7. I haven't found my "people" yet, and it is worth it to keep looking.

Reflect: Did any of the above myths sound relevant to you? Can you identify and challenge any frequently occurring myths that you have? What would happen if you didn't believe every thought you had?

In social situations, another faulty tactic I often see people try to employ is that of waiting for people to approach them first. I have a great example of a time I fell for this mistake:

I was flying solo for a work trip and as I boarded the plane, I noticed that I was one of two solo fliers sharing a two-person aisle on the left side of the plane. I noted that the other woman was about my age and had a book to read which I had never heard of. She smiled politely at me and I back at her as we boarded. I immediately had the thought of striking up small talk, asking her where she was headed, whether she enjoys flying solo, what book is she reading, etc.; however, I waited too long (per my evaluation). I spent the ENTIRE flight in my head wondering what the heck was wrong with me; "*I talk to people for a living, why can't I say hi to her? She probably thinks I'm so bizarre, sitting here with no book open, no laptop --just sitting having an internal dilemma!*" "*I should just say hi, I should remark on her book/bag/shoes/anything! Instead, I am the weirdo occupying the space next to her!*" This went on for almost two hours. I had renewed chances to chat while we were landing and while we were packing up to exit the plane, but I just sat there in silence …awkward!

My mistakes were multiple:
1. I assumed she was judging me.
2. I waited too long before "breaking the ice".
3. I judged myself harshly.

Should you find yourself in that internal dilemma situation, the suggestion I have is to act fast! I heard once that if you want to talk to someone, you should do it within three seconds to avoid what I went through. I will say that sounds like sage advice! It is also crucial that you go easy on yourself. Self-validation could have gone a long way in my scenario. I could have said to myself *"It makes sense that I'd be nervous to talk to a stranger on an airplane"* or *"She isn't likely judging me, as I can see that she is reading a book."* Another tactic for knowing what to say in "stranger" scenarios (i.e., when waiting in line with others, new social experiences, at work with newly hired employees, meeting distant relatives of yourself or your friends) is to educate yourself on current events. Regardless of where you stand politically or religiously, it is helpful to read the news so that you have informed comments to make on world events! This can be done formally by subscribing to the paper (local or national) or informally by checking a reputable news app/website every few days.

Judging is a large problem area when it comes to making and keeping quality friends. I see judgment happening in the form of disparaging self-talk, making assumptions about others, and in shooting down and judging ideas of where to meet people. The first problem, self-judgment, requires practice to change as it is a deeply engrained habit. When you find yourself judging (either judging yourself or judging others), the first task is to "catch it" by noticing that it is happening. *"I am judging myself harshly and it is leading me to think that I am not worthy. This isn't helpful."* Once you catch the judgment, it is crucial that you immediately reframe it, similarly to the myth exercise. *"I am feeling anxious and wondering if others will like me."* By describing the facts of the situation instead of adding your negative judgments, we can be free of the emotional entanglements that inevitably follow!

Skill Practice: Becoming non-judgmental

Make a list of judgments you frequently have of yourself and of others in social settings:
Example: *She looks so inappropriate. Who does she think she is?*

_____

_____

_____

_____

_____

_____

Now see if you can be more descriptive. Include what you are observing in the setting and inside yourself. Describe any emotion you might be feeling as well as any feared consequence.
Example: *I am noticing that Shelby arrived and is wearing a little black dress. I am feeling worried that my date will want to be with her instead of me, and I am feeling jealous as I believe she looks better than me.*

_____

_____

_____

_____

_____

_____

Another crucial skill to revisit in this arena is the ability to be dialectical. We visited this idea in chapter two. As we know that repetition and practice both help us learn, I am asking that you re-visit the idea with me. Recall that a dialectical dilemma is when you are experiencing the impasse associated with clinging to your strongly held belief (aka judgment or myth), while blocking (stubbornly) any potential understanding of the other person's point of view. Visually think of a dialectical dilemma as planning tug-of-war. Under the opposing thoughts, you need to write in reasons that the thought makes sense.

I don't want friends.   *I need to have a social group.*

I am fearful of rejection.   Obligation

I have interested that people have   My family is hounding me to make friends.

made fun of in the past.   Apparently, research says it is healthy.

Social settings make me anxious.

I do "ok" by myself.   I do long to be accepted and feel a part of a group.

I am "too busy."

Possible syntheses:

I can look for groups based on my unique interests.

I can meet people online and begin practicing connection there where I feel safer.

I can send out one social suggestion/invite per week and stay in on the other evenings.

I can validate my anxiety while learning how to cope.

Step one: The first step is to identify and fill in the opposing thoughts.
Step two: Drop the stubbornness and curiously explore each side. This means you have to stop clinging to the side that you feel more passionately about RIGHT NOW. Be nice to each side.

Step three: Begin a list under each thought of what makes sense about that point of view.

1. Why is this thought/point of view valid?
2. What do I want to achieve if I take this position?

Step four: Work on coming up with syntheses. These are win-win ideas in which you meet at least one goal from the list on each side. It will not always be 50/50; however, you will feel less frustration and more peace with the decision as you honored BOTH sides!

Now that you have explored where you might go wrong, you need to explore ways to get it right. The biggest need is to realize that there is no wrong and there is no right. This isn't Star Wars –Yoda, isn't saying, "*Do or do not; there is no try*"! The most important skill you will need is the skill of being willing (if you have not noticed, this is a common skill). Willingness to do what needs done to achieve our long-term goal, even if it makes us uncomfortable. I think of social situations as a game of cards: you may have a crummy hand one round and an amazing hand the next; if you want people to keep playing with you, you need to be kind, open to winning with humility and open to loosing with grace.

New Ideas:

Mindfulness During Conversations

Mindfulness is incompatible with anxiety. When you are mindfully talking to someone, you aren't allowing yourself to venture into the depths of your brain where you can find self-judgment and anxiety; rather; you are actively listening and actively responding. A mindful conversation requires you to put down all distractions, tune into the messages being communicated by the other person, and let them know that the message is being received. A mindful conversation allows for true volley of information and a bit of "turn-taking" when speaking. Leaning in, reflecting back to them with verbal and non-verbal cues, asking curious and non-judgmental questions about their experience will help. A true interest in the other person and authentic willingness to learn from and about them are also crucial. In no way does this mean that you have to change your stance; rather, it means you let them know that they are important to you and that you are open to learning about their perspectives.

Skill: Pros and Cons

An internal pros and cons of adding new people to your life can also be a wise tool, especially if you have deep-seated angst about the topic of making friends. Sometimes people have heard the message "you need to make friends" from their family for so long that they have become bitter toward the idea. A true pros/cons grid would allow you to decide for yourself what the benefits could be of having a more stable/healthy social circle. This will allow you to become less stubborn when ideas are presented of where and how to meet new people.

Skill Practice: Pros and Cons

Pros	Cons
Of finding new people	
Of not finding new people	

Planning

Planning where to find people is the third big idea. Here are some places that I have had success, or my clients have found success:

• Church (especially mega and non-denominational) and related groups

• Support groups (AA/NA/Al-Anon, NAMI, local mental health agencies)

• Libraries (book clubs, exercise groups, crafters)

• Meetup.com

• Your child's school (PTO/volunteering)

• Formal volunteering opportunities (hospitals, animal shelters, parks district, food pantry, homeless shelters)

• Get a job or a second/part-time job

• Organize family events with distant relatives

• Organize a weekly lunch date with peers from work

• College organizations

• The gym

• Become a "regular" at a coffee-shop, dog park or book store

• Adult education centers

• Cooking classes

The difficulty most people have in trying any of the above-mentioned ideas is that they have already tried one or two and it was a bad experience. I would encourage you not to write off any idea. If we couple the body language, dialectical and non-judging skills with the experimenting and attending new events …the likelihood of a bad experience goes down! Thinking confidently and having calm, confident body posture goes a long way! The Buddhist idea of having beginner's mind will also come in handy. This basically means that you don't go into an experience with expectations; rather, you go into each new experience with a curiosity and a sense of wonder. Beginners mind requires you to allow the novelty to unfold in front of you, rather than clinging to your belief that it will fail (which leads to tension and fixation on negative …thus becoming a self-fulfilling prophecy).

Circles

It seems that people have a belief that (as Heidi Klum would say on Project Runway) "you are either in, or you are out." By this, I mean that people seem to have a more and more pervasive view of friendships: that friendships are an on-off, in-out, yes-no kind of situation, and I intend to convince you of the inaccuracy of that belief system. I hypothesize that it arose with social media; on most major platforms, people request to be your friend/follower/buddy and you have the choice of permitting or denying this. What power you hold! Also, how WRONG this is …

I am confident that someone has put in a request as such and you have had the experience of scratching your chin and wondering what the heck to do! Maybe they are a distant (emotionally or proximity) relative, maybe they are a colleague that you have neutral feelings toward, maybe they are a person in authority over you (a parent, a professor), maybe you don't actually like them (frenemies, mean girls, etc.) Whatever the case, it isn't a clear "yes," "in," or "no" answer. Most people tend to permit the person to connect on social media out of obligation and then each time they see a post or interaction, those same uneasy feelings arise!

The people in our lives exist in our circles. Imagine that you are in the center of 5 concentric circles (hula hoops that keep getting bigger). I certainly would not want to share the intimacy of my hula hoop with very many people; that is your inner circle. Your inner circle consists of those people that you are comfortable sharing a bed with, sharing a straw with, and sharing your most inner secrets with. I see people over-adding to this category much as they do on social media out of obligation. *"My mom has to be in my inner circle, doesn't she?"* No, she does not. Are you comfortable with your mom seeing you naked? Do you call her first with news? Does she know about your romantic life? If not, she is not in the inner circle (and that is ok)!

Your second circle are people that are close to you, that you feel safe and comfortable with, but not AS close as the inner circle people. People in this category would be close friends and family members, perhaps your best work-friend. People in this circle could be the first people you call after your inner circle people. You can think of them as the runners-up, plan-b, second-string friends. I mean that in the BEST possible way: it isn't that they wouldn't be great friends if given the chance, it doesn't mean that you cannot become closer; rather, it means that right now your inner circle is full, and we don't have the mental energy to have more than two or three really close friends in our lives. If something happened and a trust was betrayed by an a-list friend, we would absolutely move someone in from that second tier. The first/second string friend situation works symbiotically if each person is matched up, meaning if Susie is in your inner circle, you are in hers too. If Brian is in your second tier, you are in his second tier. Problems arise when Susie is in your inner circle, but you are only in her second tier or vice versa. We need radical acceptance, and we need to move some friends around if that is the case. The movement of people closer and further is fluid and on-going.

The third circle of people include your acquaintances: co-workers, peers, classmates, neutral family members, etc. This tier of people is not likely to get a call from you when you are having bad day and aren't likely to be invited to your birthday party; however, they could be on the Christmas card list or the 4th of July barbeque list. These people induce no majorly positive or majorly negative emotions; you know a few details about their life and vice versa. You wouldn't be angry to have to share a meal with them, yet you would not seek it out. You might have the most people in this circle; that is not a bad thing!

The fourth circle of people are those you interact with regularly and do not care for: co-workers, certain family members, certain peers, or neighbors. These people leave a bad taste in your mouth for one reason or another, and you certainly do not want to nurture the relationship or move them closer. Due to the reason for them being in your life, you likely tolerate them. There has not been any major event that has led to you completely cutting them out.

The fifth circle we will look at is the group of people you actively push away. These people have either wronged you or you legitimately feel disgust for their personality. These are people that you have no interest or intent of moving into closer circles; in fact, you'd push them out all-together if that were possible. You cut off all willing contact and do not engage them if you happen to be spending time under the same roof or at the same function.

In addition to the 5 circles, I'll add outcast island. You should not send very many people to outcast island; that can make life very lonely and perpetuate black-and-white thinking. For instance: if your cousin forgot that you prefer chocolate cake and bought you yellow cake instead, he should not be exiled; however, if he has been abusive, especially if he doesn't make any effort to own up to it and get help/change/apologize, you may move him to outcast island. You have zero-contact of any sort with those you have sent there. You avoid all contact or scenarios that might yield potential contact as it would be detrimental to your mental health.

If you noticed in the discussion, people could move between circles. When you first do the circles exercise, you may find it hard to fill all 6 categories; as I stated, we tend to see things related to relationships in all-or-nothing terms. I find that people put too many people in their inner circle and too many people on outcast island; it is helpful to learn to fill into the in-betweens. This also gives us more power and awareness over who we want to be closer to and who makes us feel unsafe or uncomfortable. It is great insight to realize that you can move people further away emotionally, even if you have to continue to see them! Perhaps after this exercise, you will see how absurd the social media "in or out" mentality is! I find it to be eye opening and encouraging to complete this exercise and see how many potential connections I have in the third circle that could turn into friends if given the chance!

On the following page you will find the circle diagram. Take time over the next week or so to put all connections that you regularly have into their most appropriate place. I suggest you use pencil as you may want to move people over time.

Skill: Circles of Connection

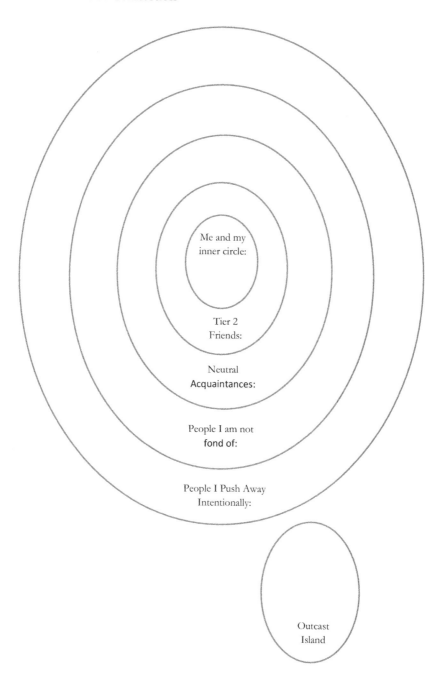

The circle exercise requires you to be in experimental mind in which you are open to any thoughts, curious about them, and initially non-committal. If you have a strong gut reaction about where a person should be, place their name in pencil and just wonder about it. As I said, I would encourage you to always use pencil for this exercise and repeat it every six months. I am confident that you will begin to see how fluidly people can move between the circles. It would also be nice for you to see when you add people to your picture (which would require you to meet new people!). As discussed in the previous chapter, DEARMAN GIVE FAST might also be a skillset to use when you have difficult relationships and when you need to be able to assert yourself to have healthier boundaries. Feel free to re-draw or photocopy the circles so that you can keep working on them over time.

8 GETTING MURPHY ON YOUR SIDE

Murphy's Law is an age-old adage that states that "Anything that can go wrong will go wrong." It is every pessimist's best bit of defense against every optimist's encouraging words. In some ways, Murphy must be onto something; I have certainly had times in which it feels that I cannot catch a break! Crises seem to beget crises; yellow snow seems to pick up speed rolling downhill in a snowball faster than clean white snow.

The origin of Murphy's Law (or whoever Murphy is) seems to be a bit up for debate. According to the book *Whatever Can Go Wrong Will Go Wrong: A History of Murphy's Law* by author Nick T. Spark, it is stated that the law came into being after an aerospace engineer Edward Murphy found that his measurement devices failed to perform as hoped in the 1940s. The other cited origin was during a press conference in 1948. Dr. John Stapp, a U.S. Air Force colonel and flight surgeon, later referenced Edward Murphy's law in a more positive light in regard to testing flight equipment. He stated that per Murphy's Law, it was important to consider all the possibilities (possible things that could go wrong) before doing a test and act to counter anything that could go wrong. In this definition, it is a preventative and wise measure to take! Perspective can make all the difference. Regardless of how Murphy's Law was born, it certainly still exists, and regardless of how it was intended to have been interpreted, it certainly has a negative connotation at present! Finance Guru Dave Ramsey frequently cites Murphy's Law as something we must PLAN for, mindfully, to avoid falling into the pit of blaming "bad luck" for things happening. The reality that we can all probably agree on is that bad things will happen in life (financially and otherwise) and we must work to be a few steps ahead! Mindfulness helps us to be awake to this reality and plan accordingly.

As I have mentioned in other chapters, I believe that we go wrong in this arena by chronically trying to avoid reality. I see people in our society that are regularly SHOCKED that they need to get gas (despite having been drivers of cars for 1-40 years), FLABBERGASTED that they have papers/assignments due the next day (that were assigned weeks prior), ASTOUNDED that rush-hour traffic exists (despite that being their daily route), and STUNNED by the April 15th tax deadline each year! These are just a few examples; take a moment and think: in your own life, what types of things do you blame others for, despite them being regular occurrences?

- Monthly bills?
- Business hours of places you would like to visit?
- Homework (either yours or your child's)?
- The connection between your weight and your intake/exercise ratio?
- The amount of time it takes you to _____ (get ready/drive somewhere/park and walk into a building/shower and dry your hair)?
- Behaviors of other people (including family members)?
- Traffic patterns?
- Weather patterns?
- Car repairs and maintenance?

I am chuckling as I write this list because: ME TOO! I never seem to recall that there is a chunk of time needed to buckle my kids in their car seats before I am actually en route! It seems to surprise me at least a few times a year that monthly bills are due every 30 days! I struggle to remember that the winter is indeed cold in the Midwest of the United States! Please don't perceive judgment from me here, I am just as likely to blame Murphy for my displeasure in these occurrences as the next person. I am guilty of avoiding reality, and I theorize that you are too.

What we need to do is avoid avoiding. We need to call our ostrich behaviors out into the open, look around, and take in the realities of our lives! If you have a traditional 9-5 job, that might mean really owning up to the length of your commute in REALISTIC traffic. If you are in school, it might mean committing to using your agenda and not procrastinating with such regularity. If you have adult responsibilities, it might mean creating a budget and sticking to it. Gone are the excuses. Gone are the days of wishful thinking, magical thinking, and hoping that when we open the phone bill this month, it will have gone down. I hate to burst that fantasy bubble, but I believe you will appreciate it in the end.

Hope is a wonderful thing. Hope allows us to envision a life in our future and dream about the possibilities, to set goals and feel a sense of optimism. Hope is a necessary agent of change as without it, we would not even try. Hope is NOT, however, a miracle worker. Hope does not change reality as it is currently happening. For example: while a high school student may hope to live in their own home, it does not change the laws about the age at which one can sign a lease. Hope can remind and motivate us to act where possible (i.e., high schooler getting a job) which will reduce the likelihood of Murphy sneaking up on them when rent comes due in the future years.

Rejecting reality is how we fuel avoidance. We frequently use it for temporary relief to life's annoyances: you might avoid someone at a social gathering to reduce your level of irritation. Avoidance can give us a false sense of security and lead to us feeling safe. This is dangerous because the feelings of safety and security can reinforce our avoidance and lead us to keep it up. For example: If I start coming in late and doing substandard quality work, I may fear being fired. If I avoid my boss, I get a false sense of security because (s)he can't yell at me if s(he) can't find me! To keep the sense of safety, you must keep avoiding your boss. Unfortunately, as you can imagine …their reasons for firing you only increase! Avoidance is rarely helpful, and for your mental health, it is not.

The goal that I want you to strive for is acceptance (a common theme in this book). Acceptance allows us to reduce our suffering by seeing what our realities really are and use our problem-solving skills to address each difficulty as effectively as we can. Acceptance may cause short term discomfort as we reveal the depths of our own avoidance (such as researching your debt and interest rates or checking the weather forecast); however, once we are aware of the extent of our current situation, we can come up with a plan that generates hope (such as a creating a budget or packing a raincoat). Acceptance does not mean that we like the reality or that we hope it continues; rather, it means we no longer choose to contribute to our own suffering. Acceptance means we will no longer try to get out of the pit by digging deeper. Acceptance means we will prioritize our integrity and our values; we will begin to set in motion a plan that allows us to live in a way that we feel proud of ourselves! Acceptance is a sign that we are willing to accept our age and our responsibilities; we are done taking risks by wishing someone will magically pay our bills, make our phone calls, do our jobs, and fly us from point A to point B (assuming you do not own a helicopter, airplane, or jet. In that case, by all means fly).

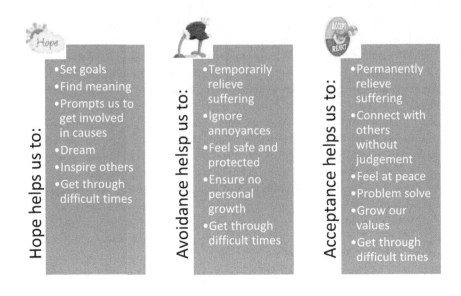

You will notice from the above chart that all three strategies (hope, avoidance, and acceptance) do help us to get through difficult times. The trick here is to choose the most effective of the three in your situation. This will be the strategy that helps you to achieve your long-term goals with more success; whereas the other strategies will only help in the short-term and can hinder your ability to achieve your long-term goals.

Skills needed:

The first skill we must remember is willingness: to do what is needed to succeed with adulting. Willingness is an attitude in which you decide you are ready and motivated enough to do what it takes to achieve your goals. Willingness may be an attitude, and it is an active choice that we must commit to if we want to see positive changes in our lives. Willingness will require consistency, too …more so than a New Year's Resolution that we scrap two weeks into January. Willingness to accept reality often includes your body language; the degree to which you commit to willingness and willing posture will dramatically impact the quality of you results! Recall that in DBT® there are a few skills that address the brain chemistry, which attacks your avoidance from the inside out by changing your brain chemistry. Half-smiling and willing hands are those two skills. Furthermore, pop-psychology and neuroscience have found that power posing and lying on the floor also change your chemistry!

Skill: Half-Smile

Even the name brings on a smirk from people; however, I want to take a moment to really explain this one...

To revisit the idea: Half-smile is NOT about faking a smile or having a Cheshire Cat/Joker-type cynical smile. Research shows that "fake" smiling is counter-productive for our purpose. If I re-named this skill, I would call it "pleasant expression." You are relaxing your facial muscles, and then ever-so-slightly putting a pleasant expression on your face (almost as if you were recalling a lovely and peaceful memory). When we use certain facial muscles, our brain is "tricked" into thinking we really are happy and it will send us the feel-good chemicals associated (Frank & Ekman, 1996)! Half smiling is so powerful and packs a big punch for being such a minor task. Paul Ekman has done extensive research on this topic which he willingly shares at his website https://www.paulekman.com/. I do admit that when I first heard this skill, I was less than enthused. I really thought "*I cannot teach this! It's so fake and invalidates my grouchiness!*" However, as I have said before, I will not preach something that I have not practiced and personally found to be helpful. I believe it is important for you to understand that even therapists and professionals have resistance to using skills or therapeutic techniques. Sometimes it just feels good to be angry!

I decided to give it a good ol' college try. I had noticed that I was irritable when I got home for work, which was interesting as I truly love my job and didn't find myself irritable when leaving work. Something was happening on the drive home that led to negative thinking patterns and ill-tempered moods. My commitment was that for one week, I would half-smile upon seeing my street sign. Every time I turned left onto my street that week, I turned off the radio, took a deep (diaphragmatic) breath, exhaled slowly, and put a pleasant expression on my face. I also did a brief body scan and worked to release any tension in my shoulders and hands. I put a post-it note on my steering wheel to remind me to use this skill (that's called a cue). IT WORKED WONDERS! I really cannot express to you how wonderful the experience was. I got out of my car in my driveway and felt calm, liberated, optimistic, and overall happy! I also need you to know that my house is only about 50 yards from the street corner, meaning this skill worked and I only had to use it for about 60 seconds (if that!). I found such peace with half-smiling that I now use it regularly. It is so liberating to realize that you have a choice regarding:

- whether or not to hold onto tension in your shoulders
- whether or not you ruminate on negative experiences
- whether or not you are grouchy
- whether or not you bring work home with you
- whether or not you look approachable

Half smiling is similar to Tyra Banks "smize" that she teaches on America's Next Top Model (there are clips on YouTube). If you watch WHAT she is doing differently between her normal face and her "smize," she has ever so subtle crow's feet appearing at the corners of her eyes, and the corners of her mouth are very slightly being tugged toward a smile. These are minuscule details; however, your body will pick up on them and adjust accordingly!

Power Posing and Willing Hands

Body language affects how others see us, but it may also change how we see and experience ourselves. Social psychologist Amy Cuddy shows how "power posing" — standing in a posture of confidence for two minutes, even when we do not feel confident — can increase testosterone and lower cortisol levels in the brain. She studied people's chemistry (in their spit) after standing or sitting in a puffed up, Wonder Woman, confident way versus their chemistry after standing in a wringing-hands, looking down, arms crossed anxious way. The change in their brain chemistry was noticeable! Their cortisol dropped and their testosterone spiked. This will have an impact on your chances for success, as it increases confidence/assertiveness and reduces fear/avoidance. I love the evaluation that Amy Cuddy asks the audience to make in the first few minutes of the TED Talk: "*Do a little audit of your body and what you're doing with your body. So, how many of you are sort of making yourselves smaller? Maybe you're hunching, crossing your legs, maybe wrapping your ankles. Sometimes we hold onto our arms ...*" I cannot tell you, as a therapist, how often I point out the same thing to clients. As stress and vulnerability go up, as does our tendency to curl into a ball and make ourselves smaller. Through her research she has found a connection to our body stance being closed off/shameful/anxious and a decreased chance of landing a job post-interview and even lower grades in college as the professor perceives you as disinterested! How you present yourself makes a BIG deal. Think about car salesmen for a moment; they approach you confidently, with broad shoulders, an enthusiastic face, and a firm hand-shake --all mannerism that communicate confidence and competence, which increases the likelihood that you will buy from them. You can employ these same skills with similar success in your day-to-day life. You can practice by walking around the grocery store with your head up and taking in the facts that you are safe and worthy of the same space as anyone else!

Skill Practice: Willing Hands and Half-Smile
We all have situations that tend to make us frustrated. For me: TRAFFIC!!!!! First, I want you to identify some common things that make you feel annoyed, frustrated, angry, etc. This could be people in your life, places you frequent, situations you find yourself in, or topics you hear about. Jot them down in the space below:

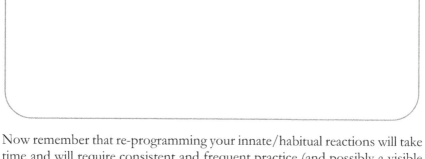

Now remember that re-programming your innate/habitual reactions will take time and will require consistent and frequent practice (and possibly a visible cue). To begin, I want you to pick one of the situations above that is on the less-frustrating end of your spectrum and begin practicing thinking of this scenario while keeping a pleasant expression on your face and having willing hands/body posture. It is important not to continue reinforcing your anger by generating all sorts of thoughts about why you hate it; rather think of the situation and try to remain neutral in your thoughts.

Example: If traffic makes you angry
       1st Practice just thinking about traffic while adopting willing hands and half-smile.
       2nd Practice half-smile while in traffic with a more neutral body posture (willing hands are not safe while driving --do not attempt).
       3rd Repeat this as many times as you can, thus reducing your automatic traffic anger!

Record your practice and experiences in your journal.

Once you have practiced half-smile and willing hands in benign situations, you can advance to practicing in more difficult situations as a crisis skill. Then you can even retrain your own neural pathways by practicing when thinking of someone you dislike. This will, over time, result in you feeling more neutrally toward them!

Wise-Minded Self-Management

As we learned in Chapter 4, time logs can provide valuable insight into how our behaviors and moods are linked. After tracking your actions and choices throughout a week, you may start to find that your mood is more difficult to regulate after 6 p.m.; whereas, before noon you make great choices and have a positive outlook. Time of day often influences our ability to perceive something as an annoyance versus a crisis. This is not uncommon, as we awake each morning with a finite amount of energy. As the day goes on, you expend that energy on all sorts of tasks, choices, communications, etc. which leaves you feeling fairly depleted as the day progresses into evening. This applies to Murphy's Law because, as we said, you need to EXPECT Murphy to be around and plan accordingly. This becomes a beautiful balance of acceptance AND change! Use the following time logs to re-track your weeks and explore your patterns. Based on your findings, you may decide to change some patterns in your own daily life.
This could mean:

- That you do not check or respond to voicemails after 6 p.m. because you are more irritable then.
- That you schedule morning workouts because, for some reason, you never seem to have time for the evening ones.
- That you don't commit to more than 3 or 4 things in one day because that stresses you out.
- That you find scheduling social time/down time to be effective.
- That you like to leave one weekend day free for errands and general tasks.
- That regularly keeping time/emotion logs can keep you "on track".
- Other_____

_____

There is no *right* answer in this exercise; rather, there will be solutions that are more effective for you. Take some time to work on this exercise in your journal. If you are not sure of your patterns, I would recommend returning to keeping weekly time logs and be open to experimenting with changing some variables. You can always try out some of the examples I shared for yourself!

Within this idea, it is important that when a curveball comes your way, do not be shocked; rather, be confident and planful. Mindfulness allows us to notice with curiosity without reacting hastily. We really do need to RADICALLY accept life's imperfections and the grey areas that exist. Only with radical acceptance will we be able to notice it without engaging in behaviors or thinking patterns that increase our suffering. Learning to build up healthier patterns and boundaries will help you roll with Murphy's visits without falling into complete crisis. This will develop your personality in new, healthier ways!

Time Tracking Log
Week of:

Time	Sun	Mon		Tues	Wed	Thurs	Fri	Sat
6am								
7am								
8am								
9am								
10am								
11am								
12pm								
1pm								
2pm								
3pm								

4pm								
5pm								
6pm								
7pm								
8pm								
9pm								
11pm								

Skill: IMPROVE

Now that we have explored how to address our actions, I would like to tie in a skill that we can use in our mind. I think of this as a bit of a secret weapon. You may find yourself stuck (in a meeting, in a line, in traffic) and unable to use many of the skills taught. I think of the IMPROVE acronym as a little secret.

IMPROVE is an acronym in the distress tolerance module. It is a crisis skill as it helps you to utilize your mind to distract yourself in a crisis, to help keep yourself from making the situation worse.

I – Imagery

You have full permission to use your imagination to mentally check out. You can imagine a safe space, a wall between you and the problem, or imagine the tension draining out of you. Imagine a peaceful nature scene that you can escape to when you need a moment to yourself!

M – Find Meaning

Finding meaning is a DBT® skill tucked in the IMPROVE acronym within distress tolerance. Finding meaning is about recognizing that you are in an undesirable situation and trying to find:

- what isn't so bad about it?
- the silver lining.
- how you can grow from the scenario.
- how we could use it as a teaching opportunity for others in our life.

Within this skill, we are not denying that the painful situation exists or stating that we like that it is happening; rather, we are looking to decrease our suffering by acknowledging the dialectic that our pain can also provide opportunities for growth. This technique requires you to be open to changing your beliefs about suffering in general. We must stop blaming Murphy and start recognizing that life has joy and pain. They require each other, for joy isn't as enjoyable if we have not experienced pain. If you refuse to experience painful emotions once they hit a 60 (out of 100), you are going to inevitably block yourself from being able to feel enjoyable emotions once they hit 60 (out of 100). You need to be able to have both to compare the two and experience joy more fully. A numb existence is not a life worth living.

P – Prayer

DBT® does not prescribe any one religion or type of prayer; rather, research shows that people who ask for strength to get through a painful situation have decreased suffering! This can be asking God, Mother Nature, your own wise-mind, Allah, Jesus, or any higher power you connect with.

R – Relaxing Actions

In a crisis, the R of IMPROVE reminds me that I can relax. My go-to choices are to make myself a hot tea, stretch, relax my shoulders, go for a walk outside, call a friend, and/or soak my feet if at home! Often, relaxing may simply include taking a deep breath and releasing the tension in my shoulders!

O – One in the Moment

When life is overwhelming, one in the moment reminds us that we can stop trying to do everything all at once and put one foot in front of the other. One in the moment can help use to stop running around in pure chaos and saying, "*What one thing do I need to do right now?*" I often make a specific to-do list and mark one thing off at a time. That might mean you commit to just brushing your teeth, then commit to getting dressed and only getting dressed. Then you would commit to eat breakfast. Slowly but surely, you will be getting out the door!

V – Mini-Vacation

This is as it sounds. What can you do to mentally check-out? Sometimes this is literal: use paid time off or a vacation day if you can leave work, go to the park or pool, go shopping, goof off, etc. Sometimes this is metaphorical: look at vacation images, research trips you want to take, make a Pinterest board of things you would like to do, etc.

E – Self Encouragement

Talk to yourself just as you would talk to a friend. Be kind, be gentle, be understanding. We say things to ourselves that we would NEVER say to a friend. Start being kinder to yourself and have an internal dialogue that mirrors the way you would speak to another person.

Reframing Myths, Absolutes, Judgments and Cognitive Distortions:

If you have not noticed yet, this chapter (book) is about you, not good 'ol Murph. What YOU do in response to the stimuli that you encounter makes more of a difference than blaming others or having superstitious thoughts. We must be aware of what we are doing in our minds and diligently fight against falling into victim mentality. Hopeless and helpless thinking patterns will pull you down every time. I refer to absolutes as "DBT Curse Words." Statements that include *always, never, just* _____, *fair, unfair, should, shouldn't, all, none, must, no one, everyone*, etc., are likely to get you into trouble as they are laden with judgment and are absolute in nature. Using those statements becomes a cognitive distortion and leads you to turn myths into facts about the world. To break free of this habit, you need to:

1. Observe that you are making the statement.
2. Reframe the statement by stating your observation only.
3. Refrain from judging yourself for making the absolute/judgmental statement.
4. Repeat over, and over, and over …

Not judging isn't as simple as keeping your mouth shut or starting to be overly positive. Not judging requires you to realize that you are not always right. Your opinion is not the same as everyone else's. When you judge *"that's great, that's terrible, she's an idiot, he doesn't even try, I suck …"* you are essentially stating that your opinion is fact, and everyone would agree. This is not true. You can reframe the judgment by stating the fact and the feeling, being descriptive. Instead of *"that's great,"* you can say *"I appreciate that you picked up dinner!"* Instead of, *"He doesn't even try,"* you can say, *"I noticed that he left practice early last week, and I had the thought that he isn't trying."*

Murphy will want you to be judgmental and make all sorts of assumptions. Remember from the first page of this chapter: frustrating things will happen —that is a fact of life. Murphy will want you to assume that it is personal; it usually isn't! When a bird poops on your car windshield, instead of stating the absolute: *"Of course a bird pooped on my window, this ALWAYS happens,"* try to step back and say, *"I am frustrated by the bird poop."* Then wash your window and move on!

Skill: Reframing Myths, Absolutes, Judgments and Cognitive Distortions
In this worksheet, we will practice how to rewrite absolute and judgmental statements into less intense language. This serves as a tool to be able to free your attachment to the topic, thus reducing your intensity around the topic. I will give you several examples. Remember: you can only observe that which you directly experienced through your five senses. You can always state your thought, perception, experience.

1. I should be able to handle my emotions better (self-judgment).
Emotions are complex, and there are times that I handle them well. I am learning to cope more effectively with more difficult situations.
2. My boss is an idiot, and he does not care about the staff (judgment and absolute).
I am frustrated that my boss scheduled me on Friday, so I called off. I am perceiving that he does not care about me, and I am aware that I cannot know his reasoning until we talk about it.
3. I hate school (absolute).
I fear failure. As school testing is difficult for me, I am nervous that I will not do well.
4. This ALWAYS happens (absolute).
I am frustrated that this happened; I am worried that I will not have time to problem-solve

the situation.
5. Expressing emotions is weak (myth, judgment, absolute).
I worry that people will judge me for expressing my emotions and I also worry that I will not be able to stop the expression once it starts.
6. People suck (absolute, myth, judgment).
I am lonely, and I perceive that if I push people away, I will feel less rejected.

Skill Practice: Reframing Myths, Absolutes, Judgments and Cognitive Distortions Cont.

Now you practice! Identify some myths, absolutes, and judgments that you recognize using and work on a way to reframe them. Tip: adding sometimes is a good first step!

1. _____

_____

myth, judgment, and/or absolute?
Reframe:

_____

_____

2. _____

_____

myth, judgment, and/or absolute?
Reframe:

_____

_____

3. _____

_____

myth, judgment, and/or absolute?
Reframe:

_____

_____

4. _____

_____

myth, judgment, and/or absolute?
Reframe:

_____

_____

5. _____

_____

myth, judgment, and/or absolute?
Reframe:

_____

_____

6. _____

_____

myth, judgment, and/or absolute?
Reframe:

_____

_____

Skill: Self-Encouragement

I want to close this chapter with a reminder of the self-encouragement skill from a few pages ago. It is such a crucial piece of the puzzle that I would like to revisit it briefly. Each chapter of this book is quite loaded in terms of content and skills; that has not escaped my awareness. This is the type of book that you could re-read over and over ...getting something new from it each time. These realities lead me to believe that you might feel overwhelmed by the information. When we are facing a task that feels unachievable or out of reach, self-encouragement can be the tool to keep us going. Very few people are successful without effort. Most entrepreneurs have failed more times than they care to recall! Did you know that the Chicken Soup for the Soul series was rejected 144 times before a publishing house picked them up?! They went on to sell 500 million copies (whereas the average published book sells 3,000 copies)!

Self-encouragement is where you speak to yourself as you would speak to a friend in the same situation. Rally yourself and remind yourself that you ARE worth it! You CAN apply these concepts to your life and see change. It will be difficult at times, and yet you are capable of persevering! What are some encouraging statements you could make RIGHT NOW?

9 SOCIAL MEDIA…IN WISE MIND

What goes wrong:

Social media is a relatively new tool to connect users with peer groups, relatives, and people with whom we might share interests. Blogging was one of the first ways to get a presence online; WordPress for instance, was launched in 2003. Myspace hit the net in 2003 and was the first site to allow people to connect, share info, and have full relationships via the internet! Facebook came on the scene in 2004 but was initially only available to Harvard, and then other college students. By 2006, Facebook was available to anyone with internet access, which was a controversial move for Facebook, as those who joined prior to then felt the rest of the world hadn't earned their place among them on the platform! YouTube was launched in 2005, Twitter in 2006, Tumblr in 2007, …Pinterest and Instagram in 2010, Snapchat in 2011, and Vine in 2013 (Thanks to David Squires @ http://scalar.usc.edu/works/everything-you-always-wanted-to-know-about-social-media-but-were-too-afraid-to-ask/history-and-different-types-of-social-media for this succinct timeline …which I did fact check!). Moving forward we now have Tik Tok, VSCO, and I am sure the list will only continue to grow!

So, the question remains: where do we go wrong? As I read through the timeline above and realize how many other platforms were not mentioned (blogger, Xanga, LinkedIn, LiveJournal, Yelp, Google +, etc.) I am struck by the fact that all people born after the year 2000 have never known a life WITHOUT social medial. People born after 2000 (herein millennials) have grown up with their parents posting their embarrassing childhood antics and publicizing their photos without consent. Even if you were born pre-2000, our culture is now engulfed by the newer, bigger, better, "next best thing" mentality. Look again at the timeline…a major platform (and let's face it…a major smartphone) is launched almost every year! This means that just as they get used to one, another rolls out. In many ways, you cannot solely blame yourself for your feelings of unworthiness, insecurity, and fear. It has been taught to you via modeling and lived experience. So, what can you do? You can WAKE UP. You can be AWARE. You can take not of the PRESENT REALITY and what your urges are.

Another significant risk with social media is the addiction that occurs because of your brain giving you a lovely hit of dopamine with each "like" you receive. Researcher Kent C. Berridge has found a very real and measurable link between your interaction with social media and your brain rewarding you with a spike of dopamine! Twitter's character limit is especially addicting due to its inability to fully satisfy, thus having you come back for more …over and over and over! Another reason the addiction becomes so ingrained in your biology (thus resulting in very strong urges) is that the reward of notifications happens inconsistently; you cannot predict WHEN they are coming, which leads to you checking often. Think of the implications that would have for someone who starts social media at age 12 …or even younger. By the time you reach adulthood, you have been "using" your drug for potentially 10 years! One simple change you can do to minimize the effects of this behavioral pattern is to turn off your notifications. You become in charge of when you check social media and hopefully, this is done mindfully. The overarching goal of therapy, and specifically DBT®, is to learn how to live without giving into all short-term urges, so that you can learn to reach your long-term goals more successfully. Do you see how practicing this skill on social media could help strengthen that muscle (figuratively speaking) and allow you to develop self-discipline in other areas? The inability to fight the urge to check our phones or scroll through social media has also been found to have a directly increased correlation to poorer sleep (no surprise there, I hope) (Kaimal et al, 2017)!

The last big area that I believe we go wrong in, is comparing ourselves to others …specifically idealizing others while disparaging ourselves. We somehow believe that we would be happier if we looked like @_____ or if we could craft like @_____ or if we traveled as much as @_____. #SNAPOUTOFIT!!!!! The grass is not greener on the other side; it's greener where you water it. To further that analogy, you reap what you sow: if you sow negative self-talk, you will reap low self-worth! Studies have found that people who spend more time on social media than their average peer have between 2.2 and 2.6 times the likelihood of body image and eating disorder issues.

To manage urges, you need to understand some effective ways to distract yourself in a crisis. ACCEPTS is an acronym that reminds you of ways to distract yourself (as not to make it worse). There will be a prompt for practice after each letter.

Skill: ACCEPTS
A – Activities
This is your typical "coping skill." Find an activity you enjoy and throw yourself into it as a break from your problematic urge or current stress. This could include exercise, crafting, hobbies, calling someone, cleaning, gardening, etc. Social medial can help us distract short-term, but we need to find other options that might be more beneficial.

What are some things you could rely on in this category?

_____

_____

_____

C – Comparisons
I can see how people would be confused as to how comparisons are HELPFUL in a situation like social media; however, accurate and effective comparison can be quite helpful. Imagine seeing someone else's success and thinking *"I am so glad that I know where to come for inspiration; I used to find photos like this and feel inferior"* or *"I can tell this person puts a lot of their time and energy into their lifestyle; I am glad that I strive for balance. I know that perfection is not the answer."* You could also use the comparison skill to look at scenarios that are worse than your life and feel grateful for what you DO have. For instance: *"I heard on the news today that a distant country is at civil war. I am so grateful that I do not know what that is like. I will pray for them/spread awareness as a way to honor them"*. The goal here is never to put down or disparage another group rather to realize that you know how to deal with the problems in your world, and you can be grateful not to be dealing with the problems in someone else's.

Skill Practice: Comparisons
What are three TV shows/YouTube channels you can watch to help put your life in perspective (in an effective way)?
Ex: *Toddlers in Tiaras, CNN, Bridezilla, The Real Housewives, Maury, Fox News, E!*
1. _____

2. _____

3. _____

Three thoughts I can practice thinking about my own progress are:
Ex: *I am so glad that I have learned how to stop responding impulsively to texts. In the past I would have started an argument; now I sleep on it before responding.*

1. _____

2. _____

3. _____

Five things I am grateful for (be specific) that I can remind myself of on a bad day are:

1. _____

2. _____

3. _____

4. _____

5. _____

C – Contributing
Find ways to help others and you will also reap the benefits. Some examples are random acts of kindness, pay for someone behind you in a drive-thru, text or send a card to a loved one, pick up litter, pray for others.
Is there a way you can help others or the environment?

_____

_____

_____

E – Different Emotions
If you are struggling with an emotion, use whatever it takes to bring up a DIFFERENT (safer) emotion. For anger: watch a horror movie or read funny greeting cards. For sadness: crank up some upbeat/intense music or read comics. For anxiety: go to the batting cages, meditate, watch a comedy

movie.
What do you think you could do to generate a different emotion?

_____

_____

_____

P – Push Away
This is done mostly with your imagination. Imagine putting your stress or urge into a box and putting that box on a shelf for now. Imaging letting your problem float down a stream.
Where can you put your worries?

_____

_____

_____

T – Different Thoughts
Similar to different emotions, in this skill you will give your brain a break from the problem by generating different thoughts. Some people have good luck with puzzles/games, some people research a topic or person of interest, some find daydreaming about an event (real or desired) to be effective.
What is a topic you might enjoy researching or fantasizing about?

_____

_____

_____

S- Strong Sensations
Use any of your five senses, intensely, to distract yourself. This could be a cool shower, a sour candy, loud music, etc.

What ideas do you have for using strong sensations to distract?

_____

_____

_____

Remember that after distracting, you will need to come back to the issue at hand and work to problem solve it!

Desire

Two of the most translated words in the Buddha's teachings are *suffering* and *desire*. That seemed strange to me the first time I heard it and now …it makes perfect sense. Desire is a strong wish/want for something we do not currently have. Desire is urging. Desire is misery. Buddhism arose from those who began to follow the Buddha's teachings. Buddha was not a Buddhist, nor am I suggesting that you must become one. What I am saying is that there is some intense truth behind what the Buddha preached about suffering and desire: all suffering comes from desire and that if we eliminate desire, we in turn, eliminate suffering. If you can work on your "Facebook Stalking" and idealizing those who are "Instafamous" WHILE working on loving yourself for who you are, where you are, and how you currently look …you would have DRAMATICALLY less suffering!!!

In prior chapters, you have learned the skill of radical acceptance as a means to work on decreasing suffering, using many of the same ideals. The basic premise here is that you stop fighting against reality which will free you from suffering. When it comes to social media …often-times the whole point for people is to deny or distort reality! Instagram has especially taken some heat for this as the filters and photos-only format frequently leads to misinterpretation of the posts. In May 2017, a survey conducted by United Kingdom's Royal Society for Public Health, featuring 1,479 people aged 14–24, asking them to rate social media platforms depending on anxiety, depression, loneliness, bullying and body image, concluded that Instagram was "worst for young mental health." In response, Instagram stated that "Keeping Instagram a safe and supportive place for young people was a top priority." The only way I have seen Instagram try to keep Instagram safe is to release statements that they are banning certain hashtags and censoring pictures they deem inappropriate. Using radical acceptance, you can uncover limitless choices within this problem. Radical acceptance reminds you not to blame Instagram, Tumblr, Facebook, etc.; rather, you have a choice in how you interact with each platform, when you check your page, why you are using it, and which platforms/users you engage with!

Mindful Social Media?

Often, you might turn to social media when in emotion mind, in an effort to regulate your emotions by activating the reward center due to that boost of dopamine mentioned earlier. This is an attempt at self-regulation and that is AWESOME! You need; however, to be mindful of the intrinsic strengths and weaknesses, helpful and harmful components of each site. Mindful use of social media requires you to consider both short-term AND long-term gains/risks. An example you can extrapolate information from is the reality that many teens/young adults are facing today: fill your social media with your real lives/thoughts …and when you are leaving college being caught off guard by a boss, significant other, even your own children finding!

Remember, what is published on-line is never really gone! We have seen politicians and other celebrities learn the hard way from this; we must be aware that we are no different. Mindfulness requires you to explore the current and future cost-benefit of the post.

Mindfulness is broken down in DBT® into a set of "what" and "how" skills. Essentially, this is a reminder to be awake to what you are actually doing (we must observe fully, describe clearly, and participate). In social media, this shows up clearly. Have you ever posted a response, gotten excited about something or angry at someone based on what you THOUGHT they wrote in a post? You didn't observe the post in its entirety, which led to you looking foolish after making an assumption? Mindfulness has us slow down and really observe the post, our emotions about the post, our urges in how to respond, etc. Observing requires a pause. Once something is observed, you can start being more descriptive. Being more descriptive will allow you to have less regrets about your social media activities. The antithesis of gossiping/being negative/complaining would be to try being descriptive. From what I have seen (and experienced), the former types of posts are the ones that will come back to haunt you; describing, on the other hand, is a bit of an insurance policy. Lastly, we would benefit from participation as a mindfulness component. That means we are fully aware and engaged in our lives! We aren't sitting on the sidelines (I see this happening on social media with people who follow a lot of topics but never engage. They get excited/angry/offended by content, yet never unfollow or assert their opinions). You can also participate in social media by allowing yourself to be fully present and post with intent …rather than mindlessly scrolling and liking things while in line for your coffee!

DBT "What" Skills of Mindfulness:

- Step back and notice
- What are you seeing, thinking and feeling?
- You cannot observe another's thoughts/motives

Observe

Describe

- Using factual and accurate words
- Start with "I am percieving..." or "It is my observation that..."
- Be open to correction

- Be fully present in your day and activities
- Interact with each experience
- Pay attention in your life and live with awareness

Participate

Let me give you an example:

A "not helpful"/risky post: *My boss is an idiot; I hate that she expects me to work through my lunch to meet deadlines!*

Less risky/more descriptive post: *I almost missed a deadline and chose to work through my lunch ...makes for a long day, AND I am so relieved to be done!*

In the first post, there is blaming, judging, complaining, assumptions, etc., all of which can come back to haunt you. The first post also would be something likely to be sent impulsively and from emotion mind. Remember that all posts could be screenshotted and sent to people (including your boss)! A third option that is even safer would be to NOT POST things of the complaining or critical nature, as those are topics best shared with close friends (in person, not on-line)! Posts that are laden with (or written from a place of) high emotion are not usually wise-minded posts. It is wise for you to check in with yourself PRIOR to posting. Observing can alert you to strong urges, desires for revenge, body tension, shaky hands, etc. I do not advise posting anything until you calm down. Wise mind can wait!

The How skills of mindfulness in DBT® allow us to remember that we need to be non-judgmental (by using observe and describe skills), aware of each moment (by being one mindful), and effective (which often requires asking wise mind what we ought to do). The how skills can allow us to reduce the risk of any backlash by posting that which would not trigger ourselves (or others), that which would not dishonor ourselves (or others), or that which would inflate any drama. Non-judgmental stance is crucial, as our judgments are what tend to cause drama in our lives. I am not saying that you cannot judge at all; rather, the way in which you present your judgment might need to change. Instead of posting *"That's so stupid,"* *"Who would wear that!"* or *"Why can't people just do their jobs?"*, I would challenge you to give us more information that we can use! *"That's so stupid"* does not tell me anything except that you're annoyed. It would be more helpful to state the fact and the feeling: *"I'm annoyed that they are re-paving the roads near my house,"* which tells us so much more! Instead of *"Who would wear that?!"* which only tells me that you are looking down at someone for their attire, try saying the fact and the feeling: *"I notice my urge to judge her for showing so much skin, and I realize that other people have different tastes. In a way, I wish I was as confident as she appears to be"*. Finally, *"Why can't people do their jobs"* is a common and very hurtful judgment as it insinuates that you know more than everyone else, you believe you are superior to others, etc. Try stating the fact and the feeling: *"I didn't leave my house with enough time to get coffee, yet I stopped anyway. The employee was doing her best during morning rush. I ended up being late to work because of my decision to stop and I had urges to blame other people."* Notice the difference in your body sensations when reading the judgmental statements vs the re-worded descriptive statements.

The next how skill is one-mindfully. One-mindfully is a reminder to be right here, right now. We often spend chunks of time ruminating on the past, which can lead to feelings of regret, depression, despair, OR we ruminate on the future which leads to feelings of fear, inadequacy, and anxiety. The worst-case scenario is someone who vacillates between the two …never fully living or enjoying the present moment. My favorite metaphor (albeit graphic) for this is that if you have one foot in the past and one foot in the future, you are in the perfect position to shit on today (insert poop emoji)! Today isn't so bad. Today isn't so great. Today …is today! In a training I attended with Marsha Linehan as the presenter, I remember her saying that *"The pain of the present moment is enough -- we don't have to make it worse."* I do not believe she intended this to be a dark and cynical statement, rather a reminder that we have a choice! You can choose to accept each moment and live it …or you can deny each moment, yearn for other realities, and be miserable!

Effectively is one of my favorite skills. It provides a reminder that while life might not be fair (much of the time), you have choices that will help you reach your long-term goals more efficiently. Let me tell you a story:

I was driving my car on a summer evening around 6 p.m. with my two daughters (ages 3 and 5) in their car seats through a small town when I see the red flashing lights behind me. Now I admit I was pulled over in the same area about six months prior for rolling through a stop sign. As a result, I was CONFIDENT that I had not done anything wrong! I had stopped fully, looked both ways, used my turn signal, crept along at 25 MPH, stayed between the lane markers, etc. I was flabbergasted that I was being pulled over! I had a small urge to just keep going; after all, this wasn't fair! I pulled over and rolled my window down, awaiting the officer to come to my door. As he approached, I was glad he didn't ask the standard "Do you know why I've pulled you over?" ...because I had no idea why he had! He quickly informed me that he saw my windshield wipers swishing across my windshield, but my headlights were not on. This, apparently, is illegal. He was nice enough to let me go with a warning, but I was annoyed! The facts of my reality were that I had just picked up my car from getting an oil change, my headlights were automatic, and it was broad daylight. I had swished the wipers to clear some mist from a lawn sprinkler. After the incident, I inspected the van and realized that the lights had been switched from automatic, which must have happened during the oil change as I recall driving the night before and they worked. Also, I am not sure how I was supposed to know that the lights were not on... given it was daylight out.

I share this story because it is a great illustration of the need to be effective. I wanted to keep driving, I wanted to have a bad attitude with the cop, I wanted to complain all night, I wanted to post on social media about it... it wasn't FAIR. Now, what you need to know about effective is that it requires you to recognize that FAIR is a 4-letter F word ...and it will only upset you, as its cousin (another 4-letter F word) is known to do. Effective means to play the hand you were dealt, not the one you wish you were dealt. I was dealt the hand of being pulled over. Consequently, I played my hand well and was not ticketed. I certainly could have ensured a ticket by acting out my anger.

DBT "How" Skills of Mindfulness:

- Be descriptive of your experience, without adding your coloful 2 cents
- Should be said in a way that you wouldn't worry about anyone hearing you say it

Non-Judgementally

One Mindfully

- Not multi-tasking
- Doing one thing at a time
- Being aware of what you are doing in each moment
- Staying in the present as often as possible

- Play by the rules of your actual life, not the one you wish you had
- Choose a willing attitude towards tasks you might not be eager to do
- Let go of anger about fairness

Effectively

Skills: What and How Skills

Take a moment to reflect on how you could apply each of the skills below to social media. Note what you are doing well, what you are not doing well, and one way you could improve.

Observe	Doing well:	Not Doing Well:	Goal to Improve:
Describe	Doing well:	Not Doing Well:	Goal to Improve:
Participate	Doing well:	Not Doing Well:	Goal to Improve:

Non-Judegmenally	Doing well:	Not Doing Well:	Goal to Improve:
One-Mindfully	Doing well:	Not Doing Well:	Goal to Improve:
Effectively	Doing well:	Not Doing Well:	Goal to Improve:

Mindful Self-Audit:

List your social media accounts (a non-exhaustive list: Facebook, Tumblr, Twitter, Pinterest, LiveJournal, Instagram, Vine, LinkedIn, Muscial.ly, DeviantArt, Flickr, Foursquare, Goodreads, Google+, Grindr, Bumble, Meetup, Myspace, PatientsLikeMe, StumbleUpon, Xanga, Yelp, Blogger, WordPress, Skype, Snapchat, Reddit, Cafemom, Nextdoor, YouTube, TikTok):

Site:	How it makes me feel most often:	Why I have it:	Why I started it:	Do I genuinely like it?
Ex: Facebook	Bored, unproductive, ambivalent	To see pics of family	In college to connect with friends	Not really

Reflect by journaling:

Based on your mindful audit (that I do hope you revisit a few times over the next week to be sure you captured your authentic beliefs about the sites), take some time to journal on the things you discovered. What are your beliefs about social media? Do they support your purpose/goal of each account? Would it be beneficial to close any accounts? Does your social medial posting activity support your wise minded values? Do you think you could put more healthy energy into a few platforms as opposed to spreading yourself too thin over so many? Is there another way to get your needs met (i.e., my example to connect with family could be met by organizing family barbecue or hangouts)? For any that you are really struggling with, you could create a pros/cons of keeping the account vs not keeping the account. Work on these questions this week in your journal.

Skill: Cycle of Emotions

The last large concept to understand and apply to adulting well with social media is the idea of the wave that happens as we experience the cycle of an emotion. Urge surfing is a metaphor for how we can cope with experiencing emotions.

The stages of the cycle of emotions are:
1. You first experience a cue (aka prompting event) which can be internal (such as a memory) or external (something we experience through our senses)
2. You then have an interpretation of that cue. This is your judgment or assumption of why the cue happened. It is your narrative.
3. Based on your interpretation, you begin to have biological experiences (changes within our physical bodies). These are not in your control -- they happen naturally.
4. You will then have urges to act (sometimes effectively, sometimes not).
5. Your action comes next. This is what you choose to do, and it can be different than the urge.
6. Lastly, as a result of the action you took, your experience will wrap up with natural consequences. These are the things that are set in motion after your action.

Luckily, there are a lot of skills we can use at each stage of this wave. Look at the image to further understand the metaphor:

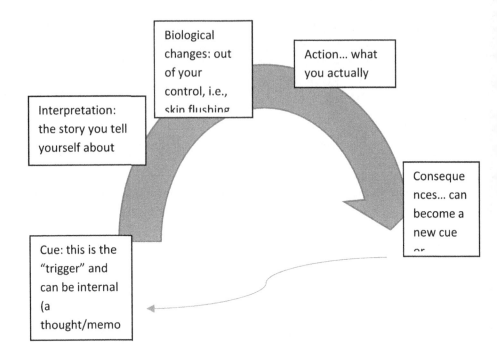

Biological changes: out of your control, i.e., skin flushing

Action... what you actually

Interpretation: the story you tell yourself about

Conseque nces... can become a new cue or

Cue: this is the "trigger" and can be internal (a thought/memo

If you think of the metaphor of your emotions as this wave, your goal is to surf on top of the wave …to recognize our urges and NOT to act, unless you are sure it is a wise-minded choice. Surfing on top of the wave can be quite uncomfortable; don't you think newer surfers are also scared when they are riding big waves? That fear is not a BAD emotion; it is a natural emotion. Unfortunately, if you do not ride the wave, you can fall into it and be tumbling around at risk of hitting rocks, being stung by jellyfish or attacked by a shark! Not to mention the discomfort of not being able to breathe/inhaling salt water! I would venture to say that the experience of being jumbled in a big wave would be sheer terror! So, you may tend to think that fear is a bad emotion; however, if you are willing to risk trying something new by changing your interpretations, you can avoid the potentially horrific consequence of your target behaviors! You absolutely need to recognize that urge surfing will cause short term discomfort, yet it opens the door for freedom in your future. Paradoxically, giving into your urges causes short-term relief; however, it opens the door to long-term suffering and increased consequences. You must make an inner commitment to do the HARD WORK that is needed to delay short-term urges in lieu of long-term rewards!

You can strengthen the ability to surf your urges by practicing in our day-to-day lives, on small situations. All skills can be likened to learning a new hobby: in the beginning it will feel awkward and you may look silly or make mistakes; however, in time, you will get the hang of it! Think about the following opportunities:

- notice your phone is flashing with a notification and don't check it.
- have an itch on your face and don't scratch it.
- try meditation and notice the racing thoughts but don't give up.
- drive in stop-and-go rush-hour traffic and ride the urge to get angry.

All these things can happen every day. All these experiences are ways that you can practice being uncomfortable, practice having urges, and show yourself that you don't have to act on every urge!

Skill Practice: Cycle of Emotions
Practice exploring your own wave with two social media or texting situations. Does it help to slow it down?

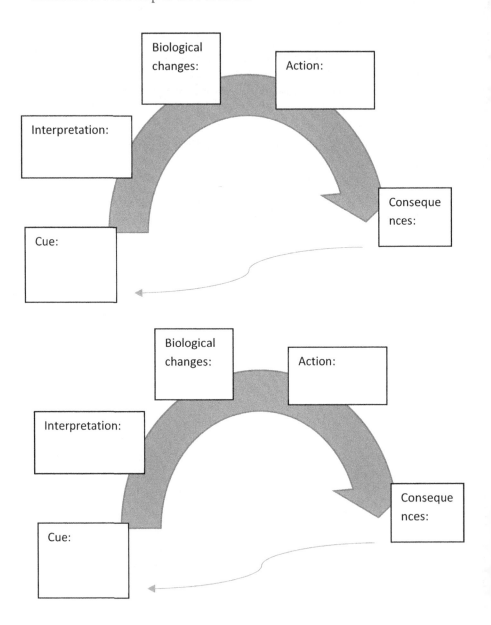

Skills for urge surfing (aka: social media life hacks!):

1. Mindfulness: Become aware; be on the lookout for cues that lead you to have urges to post. What makes you want to post in wise-mind vs emotion/rational?
2. Self-soothe: While urge surfing at the peak of your emotion, utilize your five senses to calm yourself down (i.e., lotion, candles, soft blanket, warm tea, soothing music, looking at pictures you enjoy, etc.).
3. Distract: Have a book to read as an option over mindless scrolling, go for a walk to clear your mind before you post, call a friend, etc.
4. Self-validation: Talk to yourself as you would talk to a friend. No disparaging thoughts about your emotions, urges, interpretations, etc. We live in a difficult and judgmental world. We are not taught to slow down; you are new to this and doing well to practice. Be non-judgmental of yourself.
1. 5.   Opposite action – If you want to do something vindictive or drama-fueled, try doing something kind instead. If you are scrolling to cope with anxiety, try deep, slow breathing instead. If you are seeking out content that leaves you feeling depressed, try filling your feed with positive accounts.

10 ACTIVITIES OF A DIALECTICAL DAILY LIFE

Where do we go wrong?

In general, the wrong turns we make in our daily living seem to fall into these categories:

1. Instant Gratification
2. "Shoulds"/Comparisons
3. Lack of Identity/Undefined Values
4. Overscheduling
5. Willfulness

In the following sections, I will untangle and debunk each roadblock and show you which DBT® skills can help in each context.

Instant gratification:

The biggest goal of this book is to teach you the value and benefit of learning to delay your urges in favor of reaching long-term goals. When I see people in my private practice having low self-worth, there is almost always an undertone of, *"What's wrong with me? Why do I keep doing _____ when I know I shouldn't?"* What I hear in this statement is usually *"Why can't I delay my short-term urges long enough to make progress?"* The reality is our world isn't built for that. Marketing as a field of study is all about trying to get people to act impulsively, eat more, buy faster, perceive a deal when there isn't one, etc. You are not flawed …you are human! You are doing exactly what our culture and society has trained you to do; we need to learn the tricks of companies and products so that we can have increased awareness, and consequently, decreased impulsive actions. The concept of urge surfing helps us to change our interpretation within the model of emotions.

Consider the wave of an urge that happens with the cycle of emotions from chapter nine as they relate to purchasing an item. Can you back it up enough to discover your cue/trigger to purchase, what your interpretation was, etc.? Does it help to slow it down? What could you do with this new information? Your interpretation is within your control. This is crucial to understand as this will allow you to make behavioral changes and free yourself from dependence on target behaviors and/or addictions!

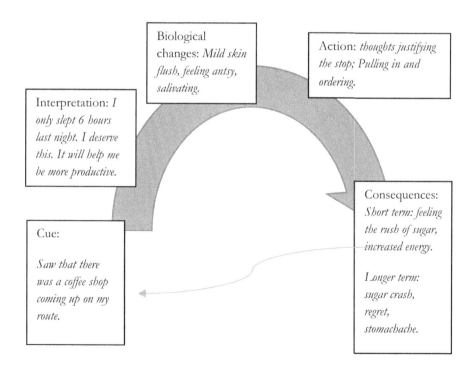

In this example, I did not do anything to change or challenge my interpretation. I allowed my decision to be mood dependent. I did not touch base with wise mind (which is almost always a bad idea!). I encourage you to always complete a second (or third or fourth) one-on-one with a different interpretation and see what the different outcomes could be!

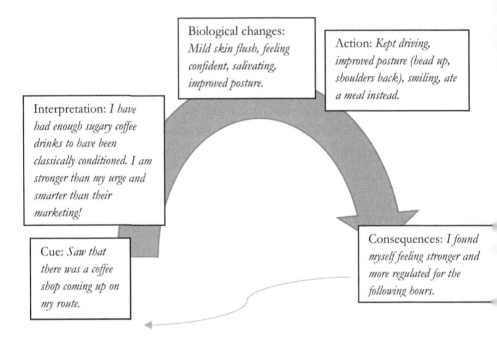

Biological changes: *Mild skin flush, feeling confident, salivating, improved posture.*

Action: *Kept driving, improved posture (head up, shoulders back), smiling, ate a meal instead.*

Interpretation: *I have had enough sugary coffee drinks to have been classically conditioned. I am stronger than my urge and smarter than their marketing!*

Cue: *Saw that there was a coffee shop coming up on my route.*

Consequences: *I found myself feeling stronger and more regulated for the following hours.*

Notice how a change in the interpretation changes the entire outcome. We have so much power in our thoughts! You get to choose which label you apply to various situations. Think about how radically you could change your daily life with this idea: what would your commute be like if you interpreted that the other drivers were rushing to get their sick dog to the vet? Instead of anger …you would end up with empathy! What if you interpreted that people who are ignoring you are stuck in their own heads trying to cope with really bad news …you would end up with concern instead of rejection.

"Shoulds"/Comparisons

Why, why, why do you feel the need to keep up and be so similar to our peers? Why, why, why do you perceive it as a threat to be different? Why, why, why do you insist that you "should" be different/better/smarter/cooler, etc.? Historically, this desire to be the same may have served us well, as being evicted from your "tribe" could be life-threatening. If you were ousted from your cave-tribe, you would die of starvation or be eaten by a sabre tooth tiger! In today's world, though, this is no longer the case. What I see is that this boils down to a self-confidence issue. If you don't feel confident enough to stand out, to be seen, you will try to blend in. The next section is what I recommend you work on to address this problem. It helps though if you are aware of this problem. You may need to take some time and journal on where you feel the pressure to fit in. Is it at work? Is it within your extended family? Where do you find yourself acting according to someone else's values?

Lack of identity/Undefined values

I am sure it is no surprise that many people (adults and teens) do not really know who they are. Remember: "*If you don't stand for something, you'll fall for anything.*" I believe this is the essence of why you may struggle with consistency in your day-to-day. It seems that many of my clients are all stuck ping-ponging from one value to another. An example is that if you commit to a workout plan because you value health …but three days in you decide that you should prioritize your value of self-care and you stop exercising, you will not reach your goal. You must learn the art of balance and consistency, which almost always requires the realization that perfection is unattainable and undesirable.

As I mentioned in the beginning of this section, you need to know who you are and what you value. You would likely benefit from going back to chapter three and re-doing the values assessment now that you are this far in the book. Your values will ebb and flow over time, changing with the seasons of your life. Re-assessing your values can remind you what you would like to keep at the forefront of your mind; this WILL influence your actions. When you get passionate about a topic and educate yourself on that topic, you are more likely to follow-through. Example: If you want to be in better physical health, your eating habits will need to be altered. Because you have decided that you value good physical health and self-care, it would be wise to research healthy eating, the consequences of unhealthy eating, the ins-and-outs of nutrition (nutrients, protein, benefits of eating certain types of foods, consequences of eating certain types of foods, etc.), and anything else you can remotely think of that could become a barrier. Personally, when I notice that I am eating a lot of sugar, I research the risks and consequences of high refined sugar intake, the effects of sugar withdraw, etc. and this allows me to skip my sugary beverage and mindfully enjoy a glass of ice water while experiencing pride in myself! Researching your values will feed your passion and promote change; avoidance of gaining this knowledge will do the opposite.

Overscheduling

As a parent, I have become very aware of the pressure to put kids, toddlers, even BABIES into extracurricular activities. The message I get from parenting magazines is that if my three-year-old is not in ballet, foreign language classes, swim lessons, soccer, AND acting classes, I am failing as a parent and the child will never succeed. Marketing is becoming quite a display of fear mongering. This means that marketing agencies, commercials, magazine covers, and new programs are playing on your fears and insecurities to sell you their item. FOMO (fear of missing out) is even a word now! FOMO is especially triggered by social media and the belief that something awful will happen to you if you miss out on ANYTHING. Now the reality of this is quite silly; you cannot possibly experience EVERYTHING …and yet you may find yourself trying to do just that! If you forgot to be mindful of what you ARE doing, you can forget that the present moment is truly all that exists. As a result, during a potentially pleasant activity, you might be in your head worrying about what you are not doing. You might try to play out a million scenarios of what you could be doing that might be more fun or more productive; or conversely, you could be in your head ruminating about how much you do not deserve this enjoyable moment or when it will end and what comes next. If that sounds familiar, remember that mindfulness is your friend. Mindfulness is a reminder that even amid an overscheduled day, you can mindfully enjoy the moment-to-moment experiences as they unfold.

What I have found personally with scheduling, is that three is my limit. Three scheduled things in my day are the maximum I will allow …two is preferred. In reviewing your own time audit from chapter four, I hope you started to see similar trends. When we have too many appointments or tasks crammed into one day (i.e., doctor appointment, work, family gathering, errands) we feel chaotic, unstable, and overwhelmed. I would encourage you to re-assess your weeks' time use using the time audit log and track your emotions along with it. You may start to see that you have a sweet spot in terms of scheduling. You may also find that "chunking" your days can help you to identify this sweet spot. This means shading in portions of your days for things like errands, cleaning, yard work, going to your job or school, family outings, etc. Once you see your days as chunks of time, you can try to alter the week to move around the moveable chunks into more effective places, such as moving errands to a day with less obligation.

Another skillful step when it comes to overscheduling is to use FAST from the DEARMAN skill, which was taught in chapter six. FAST reminds us:

- to be Fair: to others (benevolent demanding) and to ourselves (compassionate flexibility).
- to stop Apologizing when we have not done anything wrong; stop apologizing for things like prioritizing your mental health, setting appropriate limits with your time and within your relationships, needing to cancel plans due to illness, or asking to rearrange plans to be more effective.
- to Stick to our values (which you just re-assessed)
- to be Truthful.

This might mean you say something like:

"Mom, I know you want me to come help you plant flowers today; however, I am feeling overwhelmed because I have two papers to write this weekend in addition to my normal chores. Can we wait until Tuesday evening instead? I would be able to enjoy our time more if I wasn't feeling the pressure of my homework".

Or

"Marvin, I got your e-mail asking me to cover your shift next week. I am not able to do this as I have worked 50 hours/week for the past two weeks, and I am noticing that my depression is creeping back in. My mental health is really important to me, and I am working hard to learn my triggers and ways to find balance before a crisis hits! Maybe you could ask Robert; I heard him say he wants more hours. Thanks for asking me and thanks for understanding!"

The amount of information you share with another person needs to be dependent on the relationship. In the example with Stan, I am assuming the speaker is a friend and they have worked together for years. I would not give so much detail to a person in your outer circles. To a more distant colleague, I might advise saying:

"Stan, I got your e-mail asking me to cover your shift next week, and I am not able to do that. Maybe you could ask Robert; I heard him say he wants more hours. Thanks for asking me and thanks for understanding!"

Please note that there were no apologies in any of the scenarios. It is important that you are confident in what you are asking/asserting so that you garner respect and further build your self-confidence! You do not need to apologize for doing something that is right for you, healthy for you, or appropriate for the relationship/scenario.

Take some time to practice what you would say in relevant contexts of your life. Here is a review of DEAR and FAST:

D – Describe: State the facts of what the situation is. Do not include embellishments or judgments. *(I noticed that_____, or When _____ happened)*

E – Express: Tell them how you feel and/or what your opinions are! Do not assume others can read your mind! *(I feel _____)*

A – Assert/Ask: State what the request is. Be clear and keep your tone neutral. Wondering with is a good strategy here. *(I would like_____, Could you _____)*

R – Reinforce: Tell them why they will benefit from doing what you are asking of them. This is not meaning to threaten, rather to state out the positive consequences of their compliance. (*so that*_____)

F – Be Fair. Be fair to your needs and the other person's needs.

A – No Apologies. Do not be overly apologetic! We all tend to overuse "*I'm sorry*" as a sentence starter. I suggest you use DEAR and then add a "*thank you*" when they answer (if they say no… "*thank you for considering*").

S – Stick to Your Values. This requires you to evaluate your values and know what they are! Do not do things that make you feel immoral.

T – Be Truthful. Tell the truth; do not act helpless or manipulative.

Write out a few example scripts in your journal.

Remember that being dialectical means that you can see the truth in two (or more) opposing concepts. Being dialectical and living dialectically means that you can see the truth in the skills AND you can see the benefit of being flexible at times. In DBT®, we refer to this dialectic as benevolent demanding vs compassionate flexibility. To be benevolently demanding of yourself, you must be willing to seek help (Great job! You did this by reading this book!) AND be willing to try the skills wholeheartedly. You aren't just willing to try the skills; rather, you are willing to master the skills by practicing them over and over, in a variety of situations. We must bolster the motivation to CHANGE parts of our life. This might look like:

- Going to the gym regularly
- Decreasing your sugar intake
- Quitting smoking
- Willingly contacting peers to build relationships
- Engaging in positive self-talk
- Going to therapy/work/social events
- Attending church or another social outlet
- Taking walks

- Cleaning your room/home
- Reading and re-reading this book
- Attending support groups

If any of those suggestions struck a raw nerve, pay attention! That might be your body's way of showing you which things to work on. The other side of this dialectic is the realization that we must also work on ACCEPTANCE. We cannot continue to deny that our emotions exist, block our past, or throw hypothetical temper tantrums when things do not go our way. Some things you might need to work on accepting:

- Your body as it looks today
- Your paycheck as it currently is
- Past hurts
- Current political climate
- Your family dynamics as they currently are (remember acceptance opens the door to change!)
- The weather
- Your level of energy (or lack-thereof)

I need you to hear this: if you only ever focus on benevolent demanding and change, you might get a bit burnt out and give up. How many times have you started a diet or workout plan only to quit a few days in? There is also a time and a place for compassionate flexibility or acceptance. I think of this as a wise-minded way to break the rules. Compassionate flexibility allows you to nurture yourself, admit you need help, and accept that help! This means that you do not have to look or act "tough" all the time. You can allow yourself to a take day off. Compassionate flexibility might look like:

- Canceling (with appropriate notice, not in emotion mind) or declining plans
- Skipping the gym (mindfully, choosing instead a wise-minded activity)
- Allowing yourself to "veg" and watch a movie (mindfully, tuning in and allowing yourself to enjoy it!)
- Eat chocolate (slowly, taking it all in)
- Take a mental health day (not a binge-watching day)
- Self-soothe instead of powering through a situation

The interesting thing is that I just contradicted myself! I told you that you need to go to the gym AND take a day off from the gym! This is accurate, and I know that it is frustrating. This has probably happened to you repeatedly; you have probably received mixed messages in the past and felt panicked. The difference here is that you know what wise mind is, how to get into that mental state, and I want to empower you to make mindful choices about how to structure your weeks. I wholly believe that you have the ability to make good choices for yourself. If you are not sure how to respond to a request, ask for time to think! I know in the past that you have been reprimanded for your choices; you have probably been called lazy or been told to suck it up. I am seeking to empower you to make choices and keep your head held high. Use opposite action (taught in depth in chapter twelve) to address your body language and not permit shame to plant any seeds here. There is a time and a place for both acceptance and change -- your job is to use wise mind to figure out the more EFFECTIVE time to cancel and the more EFFECTIVE time to push through. No one else can tell you which one to do.

11 LONG HAUL VS INSTANT GRATIFICATION

I think you have caught on now that my goal with this book is to teach you how to delay your short-term urges to achieve your long-term goals as that is the essence of DBT®. I want to help you learn to listen to that little voice that tries to speak up when you are about to do something impulsive! When people ask me what DBT® is, I share that goal with them and almost everyone immediately agrees that our culture needs a hefty dose of this medicine. As with all medicine, it will not always taste good …AND it will be worth it. Making these changes is worth it. Achieving your long-term goals is worth it. Living according to your values is worth it! You …my friend …are worth it. Close your eyes and say that, over and over; say, "*I am worth it.*" Breathe deeply and slowly and say it again: "*I am worth it.*"

What goes wrong:

Peer pressure

Let's be honest: peer pressure is alive and well, no matter your age! I cannot tell you how many times I hear adults say things like, "*I need a glass of wine*" or "*I could go for a beer.*" We encourage each other to go mindlessly shopping, walk to the coffee shop for a $5 coffee out of sheer boredom, or promote binge-watching shows! The undertone of peer pressure is active when we shop, too! How many shirts, mugs, water bottles, cutesy pieces of merchandise can you recall seeing recently that promote drinking, shopping, or vegging out in some way?

- Namastay in bed
- Toes in the water
- But first ...coffee
- Nap first, adult later
- My head says gym, but my hearr says taco
- Tired as a mother

This is just a sampling of phrases that I have seen recently that all encourage giving in to short-term urges! I suppose a shirt that says, *"I work hard to achieve my wise-minded goals"* wouldn't be very catchy; so how can you embrace this mentality while the world is working against you?

Our big ideas to practice in this chapter are:

1. Decrease mindlessness.
2. Learn more about the hidden tricks of marketing.
3. Own your avoidance and learn to avoid avoiding.
4. Recognize when low self-esteem is a vulnerability factor.
5. Self-encouragement and self-soothe.

Decrease mindlessness

To be mindless is to be asleep at the wheel of your life. Mindlessness is being on autopilot, and worse ...not even realizing it! Mindlessness is a state of mind in which things happen TO you in your life and you can't do anything but blame others. If you were able to facilitate and build awareness, how would that awareness free you? How different would your life be if you happened TO your life? If you made the choices and had a sense of competence and a sense of worth? How different would your life be if you could see things coming instead of feeling attacked all the time? As we have discussed mindfulness throughout this book, I hope you are starting to see how crucial of a concept it is. All skills must be done with intention and awareness if you want them to work! Instead of spiraling downward, you can turn it around and promote your own life improving. Acting with awareness will reduce negative outcomes and blame. This will improve your mood, which in turn will improve your motivation. When you are more motivated, you are likely to seek out new information and change old habits. Up ...up ...and away!

To apply mindfulness and awareness to achieving your long-term goals, you do need to learn more about the hidden tricks of marketing. Marketing THRIVES on you being un-aware ...on you being asleep at the wheel. If you take a mental walk through a shopping mall or a mental drive down a busy road, think of what you would see: brightly colored sale signs, witty billboards, flashing lights, last-chance deals, iconic brand logos, etc. A sense of urgency arises which makes you anxious (although you may not be aware of this) ...LAST CHANCE ...really?! You get the message that there will not be another sale, this truly is a limited-edition item, you will be seen as cooler if you carry around an item with a certain logo on it ...but, really? Would you stop being friends with someone who didn't buy the type of coffee you covet? Do you really ask people where they got their clothing and snub them if you don't like their answers? How do you know their name brand purse isn't a "knock off"? Since I have been applying these principals to my life, I get more excited when I find something I like at a second-hand store or on the discount rack! I know it is more likely to be unique AND cause me less financial guilt.

In terms of science, studies have found that slow music induces browsing and classical music causes people to purchase more expensive items. Bright colors get people in the door, while cool colors get people to spend more. (Cain-Smith and Curnow (1966); Milliman (1982 and 1986); Caldwell and Hibbert (1999)). Think about that the next time that you see the bright red SALE sign out front and the calm, cool décor inside the store! The more you educate yourself on these idiosyncrasies of life, the more you can become aware of your influences and awake to your actions. I am not against stores using these techniques; rather, I am interested in learning more so that I do not fall prey (unless I want to!).

Self-reflection Worksheet

What have you purchased recently and regretted?

1. _____

2. _____

3. _____

4. _____

5. _____

Would there have been a less expensive way to get a similar item? What if you waited? Shopped around? Bought used?

What do notice that you fall prey to more often?

Ex: *last chance sales, electronics, new releases, yard sales, etc.*

One way to counteract the impulsive urges (financially and otherwise) is to have a five-year plan of sorts. In DBT®, we refer to this as your life worth living. Your life worth living is your plan for where you would like to end up in the next few years. It is where you want life to be and you would really believe it was worth living! As if imagining planning for a road trip, the life worth living becomes your map. You could decide, on a whim and without a map, that you want to go south …and you might have fun …but if you didn't put thought into it, you might realize once you reach Florida that you don't like the climate and deep down, you'd rather be in Oregon. Now …. we have a car and we can certainly start driving to Oregon from Florida…but it is MUCH more effective to head to Oregon first. Below, we will work on identifying your own life worth living based on your values that you explored in chapter three.

Take a moment to review this example life worth living plan, then your own.

Life Domain	One thing I do well	Three(ish) goals (big or small)
Family	*Trying to text my mom several times a week*	*1. Also text my brother and dad.* *2. Spend 1:1 time with _____.* *3. Thank my aunt for being supportive.*
Socially	*I try to say yes to social events to reduce isolation*	*1. Take the lead on the next event.* *2. Start attending a book club.* *3. Look for options on meetup.com.*
Financially	*Ex.: I do not use my credit card regularly*	*1. Meet with a financial advisor. 2. Make a savings account and plan.* *3. Contribute more to my retirement at work.*
Emotionally	*Ex.: I am reading this book and doing the exercises!*	*1. Find a therapist.* *2. Allow down time.* *3. Meditate.*

Spiritually	*Ex.: I think about God and church often*	1. *Attend church regularly.* 2. *Read Bible verse daily.* 3. *Pray for others daily.*
Self-Expression/ Identity	*Ex.: I think about how to live a values-based life*	1. *Start volunteering.* 2. *Stop all gossip.* 3. *Take time to check in with people (be kind).*
Romantically	*Ex.: I tell my partner they are important to me*	1. *Take action on kind gesture.* 2. *Prioritize date night.*
Academically	*Ex.: I listen to TED Talks*	1. *Prioritize reading non-fiction weekly.* 2. *Look into community education classes*
Other: (work, parenting, etc.)		

Life Domain	One thing I do well	Three goals (big or small)
Family		
Socially		
Financially		
Emotionally		
Physically		

Spiritually		
Self-Expression/Identity		
Romantically		
Academically		
Other:		

As you are working through your life worth living assignment, you may find that creating a vision board or art journal could be a helpful aide. Louisa Jewell has written a great book entitled Wire Your Brain for Confidence in which she brings research out of "the ivory tower" and down to the everyday person. One thing I was amazed to learn is that research shows that people who visualize working hard and succeeding actually succeed more than people who just visualize a desirable outcome. In DBT®, we use the cope ahead skill for this! In short, we visualize coping well with our situation, rather than visualizing the catastrophe that we fear will unravel. Furthermore, Louisa Jewell finds in her research in the field of positive psychology that we must believe we can succeed (we must have self-efficacy) and believe that we have the ability to work hard and achieve. This idea pairs well with self-encouragement. I like to make a visual of this concept by making collages of strength images, power phrases, and images that remind me of my goals. Hanging this where I can see it reminds me to keep at it! You could do the same electronically or in a scissor-and-tape crafty way!

Next, I would like you to take time to complete a pros and cons grid on acting towards your life worth living. Even though you have already identified a desire to change and work towards your goals by buying this book, we must honor the anxiety and fear that comes with change!

Skill: Pros and cons

	Pros		Cons	
Of working toward life worth living				
Of not working toward life worth living				

Own your Avoidance

You may find that you get into a lot of trouble when you are avoiding dealing with an issue. Coping by using avoidance is a maladaptive coping skill that many people have learned over the years. Avoidance means that you pretend that a real issue isn't such a big deal. This can be done inside or outside of your awareness; both are challenging. Your first goal is to realize when you are avoiding …and then take actions to avoid avoiding!

To do this, you need to recognize when low self-esteem is a vulnerability factor. It might sound absurd; however, an example of this comes up with debt and spending. Do you avoid looking at how low your bank accounts are (or how high your debt balances are) and go shopping anyway because the purchase provides a shot of feel-good chemicals in your brain? If you do this type of behavior enough, an addiction will form. Low self-esteem can also plant negative self-talk in your head, which can have catastrophic results. *"I'm a failure," "There's no point in trying,"* and *"I am such an idiot"* are all examples of the kinds of self-sabotaging talk that can lead you to impulsive behaviors. When you find this happening, I recommend slowing down and identifying what it is that you are having urges to avoid. *"I'm a failure"* might be a thought that pops into your head before you start a new class. This thought will try to convince you that you should avoid the class altogether. The goal here will be to break it down into small steps. Instead of viewing yourself as a failure, make a list of what needs to be done before classes start, and tackle one thing at a time! Your list might include:

1. Look at the recommended route between home and class.
2. Print the syllabus.
3. Purchase the book.
4. Gather a backpack, pens and paper, the book, and a snack for class.
5. Commit to stay for first half of first class, etc.

Accountability partner

America is an individualistic society. This means that we tend to hold certain emotional myths as facts:

Asking for help is weak.

I must show everyone that I can do it all on my own.

Showing fear or being overwhelmed is a failure.

I should be able to handle this.

The problem with these beliefs is that they are MYTHS ...not FACTS, and yet you may treat them as absolute facts about the world. Believing them leads to more negative self-talk, thus perpetuating the cycle of target behaviors and shame. Brene Brown is a brilliant researcher on the topic of shame (I highly recommend her books when you finish this one), and she identifies in her research that shame thrives in secrecy. She is the master in this field. Consider if you believed her quotes below instead of the myths above:

"If we can share our story with someone who responds with empathy and understanding, shame can't survive."

"Shame corrodes the very part of us that believes we are capable of change."

"Vulnerability is the birthplace of innovation, creativity, and change."

"Vulnerability sounds like truth and feels like courage. Truth and courage aren't always comfortable, but they're never weakness."

"We live in a world where most people still subscribe to the belief that shame is a good tool for keeping people in line. Not only is this wrong, but it is dangerous. Shame is highly correlated with addiction, violence, aggression, depression, eating disorders, and bullying."

Now, imagine if you created new mantras and new self-talk based on these quotes instead. Your self-talk could sound a little more like this:

I am capable of change.

My vulnerability will inspire others to feel safe.

I am strong enough to be honest with others.

I deserve more than my target behaviors.

LIFE.WOULD.CHANGE! Your life would become a beacon of light, a pillar of hope for you and everyone around you. Your courage to be open could cause a ripple effect in future generations of your family and friends. Remember …you are worth it. You are worth your dreams; you are worth your goals.

Part Three: Unveiling a New Future

12 WHAT TO DO ABOUT THE FEELS...

Chapter Twelve: What to Do About the Feels...

Let's change the format a bit (change can be good!) and start this chapter with a self-evaluation:

What situations are harder for you emotionally?

Ex.: *when situations aren't "fair" or when people don't follow the rules*

_____

_____

_____

_____

_____

_____

Now what makes it harder for you to remain in control of your emotions?

Ex.: *My beliefs about how things should be done; I don't know any other ways to act; Being angry feels good! It all happens so fast ...*

_____

_____

_____

_____

_____

_____

Another topic that DBT will teach you is all about your emotions! There are many things that make it more difficult to regulate your emotions, they aren't all "your fault" and yet it is your life …so you do need to learn ways to interact with your emotions differently. Let's take a look at the common culprits of what makes it difficult to regulate:

1. You don't know how – For many reasons; it may be possible that no one taught you to manage emotions. Most schools do not include emotional literacy in their curriculum; rather, they indirectly teach kids to bottle them up. Parents also were not taught emotion regulation skills; unless they sought out this information, they wouldn't know how to teach you either. This is a great example of something that might not be your fault, yet you need to learn to cope with it for better quality of life. You must put in the hard work even if it isn't "fair." If you had friends over for a party and they left your house messy, then they go home …YOU have to clean it up. You could choose to leave it a mess, but then you would suffer more negative emotions until you finally did clean it up.

2. You are too emotionally aroused – Let's face it, your best laid plans will fly right out the window when that person says _that thing_ or gives you _that look_! We all have a breaking point, and we all have sensitive buttons that our loved ones seem to know how to push. Practicing mindfulness will allow more space between the event and the emotional reaction; however, initially you need to remember that when you are at a 10 out of 10, you aren't in the right frame of mind to regulate your emotions. You will need distress tolerance (crisis) skills in that moment (i.e.: distracting with an activity) before trying to engage. Practicing mindfulness will allow for more space between the event and the emotional reaction. Imagine your thoughts as a train going past you. Initially the train cars (thoughts) all blur together and trying to jump between them is dangerous! With mindfulness practice, it slows the train

cars down and you can see that there are spaces between the thoughts and in those spaces, you have a CHOICE!

3. Invalidating environments – An invalidating statement such as "*Why don't you just*" or "*you're so sensitive*" can ping someone into their emotional red-zone very quickly. See the note on number two for how to cope with this. You need to be aware that you feel invalidated, aware that it causes you to have intense emotions, and aware that immediate engagement with that person is not wise.

4. Invisible Contracts – an invisible contract can be a belief/rule you hold toward another person (i.e.: *They should know I need help; I shouldn't have to ask.*") or a belief/rule that another person holds toward you (i.e.: "*she should know how to deal with her father by now. He's been this way her whole life*"). Invisible contracts can lead people to have expectations of one another, which often leads to disappointment or anger.

5. Biology – We know that emotional and physical sensitivities are somewhat hard-wired together. I have found in my practice that people who tend to be emotionally sensitive were/are also physically sensitive to things like touch, sound, smell, etc. Biologically, some babies are more sensitive even at birth! Have you ever seen how some babies flinch at the slightest movement of air when a door is opened, and other babies can sleep through a parade!? Being born more sensitive (some call this being an empath) makes you a bit of a super-hero in my opinion; you have the gift of being able to read a room, feel what others are feeling, and put yourself in another's' shoes quite well. This can also be a curse, as the experience is draining; DBT ® skills will help you manage this.

Function of emotions

To learn to regulate your emotions, you also need to know their functions. This will help you learn to appreciate painful emotions, as they are trying to help you! Emotions do three things for us:

1. They communicate to you – Your emotions (enjoyable or not) are signals that something is happening. They signal to us that something needs our attention.

Ex. 1: *I feel fear because I realize I made a mistake at work.*

Ex. 2: *I feel anxiety before a date.*

Ex. 3: *I feel sad when my friend doesn't respond* to my birthday invitation.

2. They communicate to others – Your emotions have a reaction in your body, which in turn signals to others how we feel. Remember that light travels faster than sound, which means people will see you before they hear you. Your body language is crucial to how people decide to interact with you; you need to learn to tell your face how you feel!

Ex. 1: *Fear leads me to hang my head, pace, and mutter to myself. My co-worker asks if I am ok and when I explain what happened, reminds me of how unlikely it would be that I get fired due to my regular work ethic and performance being great. OR Fear leads me to hang my head, pace, and mutter to myself. People avoid me because they don't know how to help, which makes me feel very alone. I leave work early and contemplate quitting.*

Ex. 2: *Anxiety leads me to be a little awkward. My date comments on this in a playful way, thus breaking the ice! OR Anxiety leads me to be a little awkward. My date isn't sure how to interact with me, and the date is uncomfortable from start to finish. We both avoid one another.*

Ex. 3: *Sadness manifests in my sitting on the couch looking solemn. My mom notices and asks if I am ok. She offers to talk with me, which helps me feel a bit better. OR Sadness manifests in my sitting on the couch looking solemn. I start to watch sad movies and cry, fueling the emotion.*

3. They motivate us – The last thing your emotions do for you is motivate you to act (often without thinking). This can be very good (such as in a dangerous situation) or very problematic (such as when we yell at someone without thinking). Your emotions can give you the push you need to take the necessary actions in life.

Ex. 1: *Fear of being fired pushes me to own up to my mistake with my boss. This garners respect and he forgives my mistake. It also prompts me to work hard to remedy the situation, which I can do once I talk it out with my boss and reduce my shame.*

Ex. 2: Anxiety leads me to put effort into my appearance and hygiene, which leaves me feeling more confident. I can flirt successfully!

Ex. 3: My sadness reminded me how important my friend is to me. I decided to call her and ask why she hadn't responded, and it turns out she was waiting to hear from her family about when their vacation plans were. She was worried I would be mad, so she didn't want to tell me until she knew for sure.

Without basic emotional understanding (emotional IQ), you are apt to blow in the wind like a paper bag, always letting the emotion dictate where we go, what we think, and what we do. This is exhausting and can lead you to have a not-so-great reputation and/or not-so-great self-esteem. People might avoid telling you things or avoid you when they perceive you are emotional because they don't know how to help. You might also start avoiding things/people/places that induce emotions because you don't know how to cope. In the rest of this chapter, we will look at how to cope with <u>all the feels</u>!

What goes wrong?

A list of what goes wrong with emotion regulation might be limitless! As we already looked at, not appreciating where our deficits came from or why our emotions are helpful will limit your insight into coping better. Society tells you not to be sad, not to worry, and certainly (especially for females) not to express anger. In a comprehensive study exploring cultural implications related to emotions and emotional experiencing from 2016 by Nangyeon Lim, it was found that Western Cultures (America) place more emphasis on high-arousal emotions (i.e.: happy, angry, enthusiastic, frustrated, anxious) and Eastern Cultures (China, Japan) place more value on low arousal emotions (contentment, depressed, calm, bored). This trend is groomed starting in early childhood, based on the types of activities parents praise their kids for and enroll their kids in. In Western Cultures, we are more apt to put our kids in sports like football and basketball (and adults model aggression on the sidelines!). Eastern cultures are more apt to put their kids in martial arts, piano lessons, etc., and demand focus/concentration. The same study also found that over a person's lifetime there is correlation between high-arousal emotions and physical health complaints more so than with low-arousal emotions. I see this with my clients: they tend to have more medical problems than the general population. Intense emotions are draining! Understanding this can allow you to train yourself to begin appreciating more low-arousal emotions and reduce our number of headaches and stomach aches! The goal is not to block your feelings and become stoic; rather, it is to experience them without egging them on and making them bigger than they need to be.

An example of this may come from anger. Consider what happens to you when you are stuck in a very lengthy traffic jam. Let's say it adds 30 minutes to your 30-minute commute and you are now going to be late. You sit in your car fuming and feeding into your angry/anxious thoughts about the catastrophes that will occur because of this traffic. Your blood pressure spikes, your stomach hurts, you develop a low-level headache. Upon arriving to work (FINALLY), you tell everyone about this traffic jam with added expletives, hand gestures, and colorful details. Your blood pressure stays high and your headache grows, and to make matters worse, you now have diarrhea and the beginnings of a migraine. Employing the components of mindfulness instead would have reduced your suffering.

The choice to be skillful and practice mindfulness has been linked to decreases in irritable bowel syndrome (Blanchard et al, 1992), improved treatment outcomes for patients with psoriasis (Kabat-Zinn et al, 1998), improvement in a range of symptoms for those with multiple sclerosis (Mills et al, 2000), significant improvement in diabetes glucose levels (McGinnis et al, 2005) and significantly improved outcomes for cancer patients, which include decreased mental health problems, decrease confusion, and a decrease in medical symptoms such as gastrointestinal problems (Speca et al, 2000). I could keep citing articles, as the medical benefits found from meditation and mindfulness seem to be limitless; I hope this is enough to spur your thought process and motivate you to at least start small! It is amazing to realize how big a role you can play in decreasing your own suffering!

I am introducing you to some skills in each chapter; they can all work together and complement one another once you learn them to improve your quality of life. This is going to be a longer chapter, with a lot of skill ideas and suggestions. Once we learn to respond to our emotions differently, we keep them regulated and are much less likely to get into a crisis! Some DBT® skills that I believe help the most in the regulation of emotions are:

- STOP Skill
- Cope ahead
- Mindfulness of emotions
- Please and ABC to reduce vulnerabilities
- Opposite action to reduce intensity (page per each main one)
- Meditation

Skill: STOP

This is one of the newest skills in the newest edition of the Linehan Skills Training Manual, and I am frequently hearing how much of a game changer it is! It also reminds me of that quote from Shakespeare's A Midsummer Night's Dream: "*And though she be but little, she is fierce.*" The stop skill is meant to help you remember that you always have choices in what you do!

S – STOP!!!!! Realize your emotions are getting to a dangerous level and freeze! This would be like if you happened upon a deer in the woods. The deer will instinctively freeze because it senses you are there and does not yet know if you are a threat.

T – TAKE A STEP BACK. If it is possible, I want you to literally leave the situation. You could (gently) excuse yourself by saying "I want a moment to think of how to respond; I am going to step outside and think for a few minutes" or "That was a powerful point you just made; let me sleep on it and get back to you." If you cannot leave the situation, you can mentally take a step back by closing your eyes and taking a few slow, deep breaths.

O – OBSERVE. Just like that deer in the woods, you need to pause and notice what you are experiencing: body sensations, urges, thoughts, body language, etc., AND observe your environment: how are others acting? What is expected of you right now? Is there a way to take a break from the situation?

P – PROCEED MINDFULLY. I love this. Proceed mindfully honors the fact that you need to do something. It also honors the fact that if you slow down, you might realize you have more choices than you first thought. The deer can choose to turn and run or to resume whatever it was doing. If you are in an argument, do you see how freeing and wise it might be to proceed mindfully by saying, "*I notice we are both really passionate about this. I would like to take some time to think over the points you made. Can we meet up Wednesday to discuss it?*" Or you could proceed mindfully by noticing your professor/boss just triggered you with a comment, and that it is your trigger (meaning they did not intentionally set out to hurt you) and you decide to take 5 slow, deep breaths and then return your attention to the lecture (thus staying in the interaction and not drawing unnecessary attention to an accidental situation).

The STOP acronym has been a great reminder for me in everyday situations like traffic and dealing with family stresses. In traffic, I can remind myself that getting upset will only harm me; it will not cause the traffic jam to disappear. I proceed mindfully by taking a few deep breaths, relaxing my facial and shoulder muscles, and putting on an audiobook! In family situations, I remind myself that everyone is doing the best they can and that I do not know what the previous 12 hours held for them. Their crabbiness might make perfect sense! This allows me to "shake it off" and stay in the conversation.

Common examples for use:

- Verbal disagreements
- Feeling judged
- Prior to sending the e-mail
- Urges to purchase items impulsively
- Traffic
- When paying bills
- Before deciding whether to say "yes" to a request

Skill: STOP

Take a moment to copy the difficult situations you identified on the first page of this chapter.

_____

_____

_____

_____

_____

_____

If you were in your wisest mind and applied the STOP skill, how could the above situations look differently?

Skill: Cope ahead

We already looked at the cope ahead skill in chapter five; however, I believe it is always easier to learn in multiple contexts so we will look at it again. The cope ahead skill is one that you would apply when you are anxious about an upcoming event that is likely to happen. Cope ahead allows you to practice in your mind handling the stressful scenario well; that is, you demonstrated in your mind that you know what to do and how to do it. Public speaking is a great example! As humans, we tend to be good at playing out the worst-case scenario in our minds. A major problem is that this can become what is known as a "self-fulfilling prophecy." A self-fulfilling prophecy is when you think something bad will happen and you ruminate on it for so long, that it increases the likelihood that it will happen! Cope ahead is the exact opposite. So instead of imagining that you get up in front of the group and stutter, forget your lines, cry, etc., I ask that you stand up and practice giving your speech in its entirety and with confidence. I also encourage you that you imagine struggling (forgetting a line, looking down, stuttering) and then you imagine coping WELL with that issue. Cope ahead might raise your discomfort because it suggests that you imagine it is actually happening (not that you are talking to another person about it or watching it on a show). The anxiety that you feel during this practice will empower you to feel confident in managing it in all other areas of life! Once you finish the practice, you need to use calming skills to re-regulate yourself.

During the imaginary practice, it is wise to identify and then imagine that you are using skills effectively. Let's practice on the next page.

Skill: Cope Ahead

On the next page I want you to identify what to practice coping ahead for, what skills to imagine using, and what the practice was like afterward. The real practice happens in your mind, in real time:

The situation that makes me anxious:

Example: need to tell my girlfriend that she hurt my feelings

Skills I could use in real life to help it go well:

Example:

1. Write out and practice DEARMAN

2. Willing hands

3. Validate her points

How I feel after practicing:

Example: more confident, more appreciative after thinking of things to validate

Now you try on two situations that are likely to occur and causing you stress:

The situation that makes me anxious:

Skills I could use in real life to help it go well:

How I feel after practicing:

The situation that makes me anxious:

Skills I could use in real life to help it go well:

How I feel after practicing:

Mindfulness of emotions

The third skill to help you regulate your emotions is to become mindful of them and to practice mindfulness of emotions by feeling your feelings. You have to learn that you can ride the wave, the natural rise and fall, of your emotions. If you continue to run away at each wave rising, you will continue to become MORE sensitive to your painful emotions. I know this might feel overwhelming; however, not allowing our emotions to have their natural rise and fall will only cause them to grow and bubble to the surface with more vigor than before. It's like trying to hold a beachball under water! If you recall from chapter nine, our emotions follow a fairly typical and observable path as you experience a prompt. Once you interpret the experience and have the rise of the emotion, it WILL crest and begin to fall. The great news about this is that it is predictable, and it will happen if you let it. The bad news about this is that at times it will be painful and scary for you. Human behavior has taught us to avoid things that cause us pain. If you have ever burnt your thumb while taking something out of the oven, you know that you will be more aware of the risk next time. Unfortunately, with emotions this process causes more problems than you had in the first place because we become more and more phobic of experiencing emotional pain!

As a result of this pain-avoidance tendency our culture has, I believe one of the best lessons I can teach you is how to struggle. Recent decades of parenting and the education system have seen the opposite. There has been a rise in participation trophies and parents rushing in to rescue their kids (of all ages) from adverse natural consequences. Martin Seligman conducted studies in the 1970s and 1980s on learned helplessness that determined the benefit of self-esteem. As a result of these studies and the 1990s, it was assumed that you could just GIVE a child self-esteem (participation trophies), regardless of whether they earned it. We are now finding that this practice has damaged people's self-worth and left us with one of the least resilient cultures and emotionally sensitive generations in American history (Seligman, Reivich, Jaycox, & Gillham, 2011). Learning to struggle through a situation, to learn the hard lessons of life, to even fail occasionally is the secret to building self-esteem and more resilient mental health. You can do this by allowing your emotions to wash over you, allowing them to rise and to fall. Feeling your feelings is a skill that requires practice.

In DBT®, I teach this resiliency via the concept of being mindful of our emotional experience. It offers a sort of bridge between crisis zone and emotion zone. It teaches us that we can learn to tolerate more and more emotional discomfort instead of the afore-mentioned strategy of avoidance, which teaches us to be more and more sensitive. Be patient with emotions; they will pass if you let them.

Think for a moment about the following emotions of anxiety, sadness, and anger. They exist on a spectrum. A low-level sadness is not the same as a mid or higher-level sadness, and yet we have been taught to lump them into one static experience. Mindfulness of emotions is a skill I would encourage you to use on low and mid-level emotions initially, trusting that you will be able to experience more and more intensity over time. If you get too overwhelmed and feel like you are entering a crisis zone, use a few crisis/distraction skills to regain composure AND THEN RETURN TO EXPERIENCING THE EMOTION. Remember: this is a very under-developed muscle for you; it needs to be exercised! You may experience frustration as you struggle with the concept. This is completely normal and not at all a sign that you're unable; rather, that you are unpracticed. It reminds me of a time that I was working with a personal trainer at my gym. He was trying to teach me how to do a proper "row" exercise. He kept telling me to contract a certain muscle between my shoulder blades. I spent MONTHS feeling defeated, angry, hopeless, stupid, inept, etc., because I was convinced that I did not possess this muscle! I could not figure out, for the life of me, what he was talking about. After MONTHS (literally) of struggle, he dug his thumb between my shoulder blades, and the muscle was discovered to me! I was so excited! I will tell you that the muscle did not spontaneously appear; it was always there. I had to practice and struggle to find it. I had to trust that he knew what he was talking about. I had to really sit with my feelings of anger and hopelessness. Please trust the process; it is possible!

This skill set will teach you to learn how to appreciate your emotions. If you have not seen the Disney movie Inside Out, I'd encourage it! Inside Out really highlighted the reality that each emotion is necessary, important, and loveable in a way that we aren't typically taught. The movie can help you appreciate unpleasant emotions, as they are often trying to help you!

In the following thermometer images, I want you to consider for you how the emotion is experienced and imagine that the intensity is very high at the top and very low at the bottom. Jot in words that come to mind about your personal experience at any level. You may want to rearrange some of the words to fit your experience. Please note that your crisis zone can be lower for some emotions than for others. For example: you may be unable to cope effectively with sadness once it raises to the level of "flat," but you can cope well with anger until it hits "hostility." Shade YOUR crisis zone for each emotion in red. Over time, your crisis zone will get smaller!

Terror	Despair	Rage
Panic		
	Hopeless	Hostile
Freaking Out		
Fear	Depressed	Pissed
Anxiety		
	Lonely	Angry
Fixation		
Rumination	Pessimistic	Ticked
Nervous		
	Flat	**Mad**
Worry		

PLEASE and ABC to Reduce Vulnerabilities

You may have noticed in the charts on each emotion, that it is harder to use skills as you go higher on the scale; often-times you do not realize (we aren't aware that) you need to use skills until you are "too far gone." At that point you may give up before really trying skills with strong effort. One way around this hang-up is to attend to your vulnerability factors on a regular basis. A vulnerability factor is a stressor; they are the metaphorical straws that build up and result in the poor camel's broken back. I'd bet you can usually handle a few vulnerabilities on any given day; however, when "one more" thing happens, you may escalate quickly. People spend years working on problem solving "that last straw;" however, I challenge you to take care of the camel and its saddle first. If you attend to your daily vulnerabilities, it is likely you will have a force field around yourself that keeps you safe from completely melting down!

The DBT® skills for reducing your vulnerabilities come in the form of an acronym: ABC PLEASE. I really believe that if every person prioritized these suggestions, our world would function with more harmony and less hatred! The skills within this acronym hold great power in their ability to keep you regulated, grow your healthy identity, and increase your self-esteem.

A – Accumulate positives (long and short-term)

Short-term: This one is simple: have fun each week! If you look at your calendar and see nothing enjoyable, your mood will likely dip. The further it dips, the longer it will take to rebound. Accumulating positives, as a skill, encourages you to mindfully choose to put enjoyable time on your calendar and then actually show up for that time, both physically and emotionally. Mindful fun encourages you to turn off the worries about your to-do list and intentionally throw yourself in! This type of fun can be simple and free. Examples could include:

- Taking a pampering bath/shower
- Going for a 5–10-minute walk at any point during your day
- Playing with your pet

- Allowing yourself to go shopping on your way home/on lunch
- Eating a meal with no distraction
- Watching a guilty pleasure show or channel you follow on YouTube
- Coloring
- Crafting/creating
- Calling/Texting/Meeting up with a friend
- Visiting local "staycation" spots in your town
- Driving with the windows down and your favorite feel-good music turned up
- Listening to an audiobook or music
- Eating chocolate or candy
- Stopping at a park/lake to just sit and observe
- Going to a museum
- Swinging on swings
- Taking photos
- Volunteering at an animal shelter
- Gardening
- Doing a puzzle
- Looking at old photos
- Other: _____

Long-Term: To identify and plan long-term positive events, you may need to revisit your values assessment in chapter three. As discussed there, a life worth living requires you to live in accordance with your values. Values-based living takes time and planning …and is well worth it! I am re-inserting the values assessment and worksheet for you to do again, in your newest state of wise mind!

Skill: Values Assessment

Read through the values list below and circle or highlight the ones that really stand out to you. If you don't know what they mean, please Google it! Also feel free to Google "values list" as there are a plethora of lists out there and you may find some values that I did not include!

- Authenticity
- Achievement
- Adventure
- Altruism
- Authority
- Balance
- Beauty
- Belonging
- Boldness
- Compassion
- Challenge
- Community
- Contribution
- Creativity
- Curiosity
- Determination
- Enjoyment
- Fairness
- Faith
- Happiness
- Honesty
- Humor
- Independence
- Influence
- Inner Harmony
- Integrity
- Justice
- Kindness
- Knowledge
- Leading by Example
- Learning
- Love
- Loyalty
- Meaningful Work
- Optimism
- Peace
- Personal Growth
- Pleasure
- Popularity
- Recognition
- Respect
- Responsibility
- Security
- Self-Respect
- Service Work
- Spirituality
- Stability
- Success
- Status
- Trustworthy
- Wealth
- Wisdom

With accumulating long-term positives, you can take your top values and break them down into goals, then action steps …thus increasing the odds that you are able to make choices that support your values. When you do this, your self-esteem and self-worth INCREASE, thus decreasing the likelihood that you will turn to behaviors that are in contrast with your long-term goals. That last line is a loaded statement. I theorize that most of us strive to feel good about who we are and the choices we make. Low self-esteem comes from consistently doing things that do not support your values, and that is often simply because no one has ever taught you to ponder your values and act accordingly. Our culture very much encourages the opposite: instant gratification and do what feels good whenever the heck you want to!

In the next exercise you will see the steps necessary to break things down into manageable tasks.

Skill Practice: Values Assessment

What are your top three values?

_____

Now pick ONE to work on

_____

Why is this the one you chose?

_____
_____
_____
_____

What is a measurable goal related to your value?

Examples:

• *With the value of competence, the goal may be to read one book per month (or listen to one podcast per week) on a topic that you want to be competent in.*

• *With the value of adventure, the goal may be to explore all the National Parks in America over the next 10 years.*

• *With the goal of optimism, the goal may be to begin a gratitude journal.*

My goal is/My goals are:

_____
_____
_____
_____

We are not done. This is as far as most people get on their own but think about it; the goals are still so big and might feel unattainable. This leads to INACTION because it seems too hard to achieve. You might then experience an increased risk of engaging in target behaviors (in DBT® we call the behaviors we want to work on increasing or decreasing our "target behaviors"). Next, we need to break it down into baby steps!

Examples:

• *With the goal of reading one book per month, baby steps include: getting a library card, finding a local discount bookstore, finding a reading nook in your house or a local coffee shop that you could read in, set up a reward chart.*

• *With the goal of visiting all national parks, baby steps include: print out a list of all national parks, begin to group them into regions, break it down by drivable trips and air travel trips, create a mock schedule of trips over the next 10 years.*

• *With the goal of gratitude journaling, baby steps include: finding a journal and pens you like, blocking out time to reflect each day, create a reward system for yourself.*

Here are my baby steps:

_____

_____

_____

_____

_____

Great job!!! I am so proud of you for working though this; I am sure it was difficult. This is an example of doing the hard work and delaying gratification to meet your long-term goals.

One baby step I can tackle now is:

_____

B – Build Mastery

This is one of my favorite skills for building an identity and self-worth. To build mastery, you are asked to think of one thing you could get better at and develop achievable steps towards this growth. If you find that you are paralyzed by inaction or that you tried to take too big of a step, break it down smaller; do not give up! If you find the steps are too easy and therefore not motivating …challenge yourself to go onto the next few steps quicker; do not give up! See the grid below:

Task Is:	Result:
Too easy	Give up, *"this is stupid"*
Difficult, yet achieveavle	Pride, accomplishment, sense of satisfaction
Too difficult	Give up, *"this is stupid"*, feel defeated and worse about yourself

Our goal is to work for tasks that are difficult, yet achievable. We see examples of building mastery in most movies. We root for the underdog to try, fail, try, persist, try, and achieve! If movies fell into either the first or third type, we would not likely watch them for long. See the following examples of tasks being placed in all three categories:

Example 1:	Example 2:
Don't clean house at all	go to the gym or exercise at all
Commit to tidying up one room/area	Commit to one walk at home and one fitness class at gym each week.
Clean the whole house in one day, including floors and windows	*Sign up for a marathon without training*

Are you able to see how we don't feel good about ourselves or have great self-talk if we stick to the first "too easy" box, we can act and have more self-encouragement in the middle "difficult, yet achievable" box, and we feel worse about ourselves if we jump to the last "too hard" box? This is not to say that you will not achieve the last box; I believe you can! I also believe you will achieve that last box faster if you have a lot of small goals instead of one huge goal!

Skill: PLEASE

The PLEASE Skill is one that I lovingly refer to as the "preschool" skill because we all know how and why to do the following suggestions, yet rarely do them with consistency! The PLEASE skill will help you to build a firm foundation for your life worth living, instead of trying to add on to a house built on sand!

P – Physical wellbeing

For this letter, we ask that you follow medical advice to care for your physical body. Take prescribed medications and take them as they are prescribed. Do not ignore symptoms! I notice that moms are notoriously bad at this …always putting other people's needs before their own. Please remember that if you don't take care of yourself, you won't be able to help others!

L – Lather, rinse, repeat (my spin on this letter)

I have noticed over the years that hygiene is one of the first things to suffer when one's mental health is deteriorating. Conversely, showering and wearing fresh clothes goes a long way toward improving one's well-being and sense of self. Get up, get clean, and get dressed on purpose. This skill is not about being fake or trying to "fit in;" rather, it helps you to feel more confident and walk a bit taller in whatever types of clothing YOU choose!

E – Balanced eating

I am going to keep this one intentionally vague because it will vary depending on person/health/lifestyle. You need to be honest with yourself about what foods are helpful and which are harmful for your physical and mental wellbeing. This skill does require mindful assessment and tuning into how your body feels before, during, and after eating different types of foods. For example: when I am tired, I crave candy. When eating candy, I feel great! After eating candy, I almost always have a headache.

My office shares a parking lot with a certain popular coffee chain. I am not going to lie; I really enjoy this perk at times. What really hurts my heart though, is when my clients show up with blended (coffee) SUGAR drinks. Here's the deal: The World Health Organization currently recommends 25 grams of sugar per day MAX. This means …you do not need to get to 25 grams. There are no bonus points for consistently getting to 25 grams; it is the red line to STAY AWAY FROM. The major problem is that most people surpass that number daily. What science knows about the consumption of added sugar in a diet (I'm not talking about fruit here …) is that it leads to your blood sugar spiking and then crashing. The effect of this on the human body is extreme. I will spare you the details other than it leads to a (short) burst of energy followed by a significant dip in mood: increased depression, anxiety, and irritability. You can use your imagination on what this looks when you repeat the cycle several times per day. A 2014 study by Emory recently found that teens with high fructose diets tend to have increase rates of depressive behaviors. Furthermore, a 2012 study from UCLA found that high fructose corn syrup LITERALLY slows brain function, impairs memory, and inhibits new learning (Agrawal & Gomez-Pinilla, 2012). So, when you are walking around high on sugar, you need to know that you are primed to NOT retain what you are trying to learn.

For your reference, here are some common sugar contents:

- Starbucks Grande Vanilla Bean Frappuccino 57 grams of sugar
- Dunkin Donuts Medium Caramel Iced Coffee 37 grams of sugar
- 20 oz Coca Cola 65 grams of sugar
- 20 oz Mountain Dew 77 grams of sugar
- Arizona Iced Tea 72 grams of sugar
- One package of Skittles 47 grams of sugar
- 2 Pop Tarts 34 grams of sugar

A – Avoid drugs and alcohol.

An easy way to motivate yourself into abstaining from drugs/alcohol is to remember that most of the time using alcohol or drugs will turn the volume UP on what you already feel. If you drink because you are sad, you will feel MORE sad. If you drink because you feel angry, you will be FUMING; researchers have found in numerous studies that alcohol increases aggression. They believe this is from a secondary problem, that acute alcohol intoxication causes people to misread facial cues, therefore increasing misunderstandings (Atwood & Munafò, 2014)! Furthermore, studies find that regular use of cocaine, marijuana, and alcohol negatively effects users' fluency, reasoning, decision making, and memory and that 70% of people who regularly use multiple substances show significant deterioration in memory, planning, and reasoning, while also struggling to identify negative emotions such as disgust, guilt, fear, and shame (Fernández-Serrano et al, 2010). I encourage people to abstain from drugs and alcohol for their first year of DBT®. You can think of it as a big experiment; we need to control the variables! You can attend substance abuse support groups regardless of whether you believe you are an alcoholic or addict; we need a supportive community of people around us and having sober supports is a great idea!

S – Sleep

Let's be real: you need more than six hours of sleep. For teens and young adults, you need 8-10. For the more matured brain, 8 is the recommendation. For those with trauma, chronic pain, or those in school, I suggest closer to 9, as that is what your brain needs to heal and to transfer information from short-term memory to long-term memory. A 2007 study by Kaneita et al. has confirmed that the mental health of those who sleep 7 hours or less per night is measurably poorer than those who sleep between 7-9 hours. I have found that my happy place is around 8.5 hours. It has also been found that poorer sleep leads to both cognitive and mental health decline in adults. The implications on this are that you will not be able to learn as easily or remember things as quickly if you are chronically sleep-deprived (Anderson & Bradley,

2013). I think you deserve to set yourself up for success! You may find it helpful to repeat your time audit from chapter four to see what your actual sleep schedule is. There are also several apps and digital devices that help record sleep.

E – Exercise

For this portion, I suggest regular exercise. Chekroud and other researchers found in 2018 that in surveying 1.2 million Americans, any type of exercise (although team sports and cycling were at the top) utilized by participants a few times per week resulted in fewer "mental health days" and fewer negative mental symptoms. While medial often discuss the benefits of exercise on depression, it is notable that in 2013, Anderson & Shivakumar confirmed a powerful decrease in symptoms of anxiety if a person exercises with regularity!

If there is a type of exercise you enjoy, you might find that exercise can be a part of accumulating positives (bonus!). If you are new to exercise, it can become something that you build mastery in (bonus!); there is no rule against double dipping on skills! Exercise can be a great way to take a break! Pop those ear buds in and go for a walk!

Skill: Opposite Action

Now that you know some ways to build up your protective barrier to keep your emotions from spiking in the first place with ABC PLEASE, you need to learn what to do when they do spike. As you are developing a better understanding of your emotions (separating them out, understanding how they are experienced at different intensities, differentiating crisis level emotion vs non-crisis), it is important to know what to do with them if they do crest. DBT® is behavioral in nature. This means that we try to target your behaviors/actions as much as possible. Remember that your behavior will influence the emotion and urges that follow. Think of your behavior as the train engine; if it takes a turn …the train cars will follow! Opposite action is a skill that helps us make a hard turn, sometimes even a "U-turn" when you notice your urges or emotions are going in a non-productive direction. Opposite action is a skill that will help you to be aware of your urge/emotion and then be able to use the STOP skill to determine in what way to proceed.

Opposite action will reduce the intensity of the problematic emotion you are experiencing. I recommend you employ this skill when you realize that your emotion isn't productive, effective, or the urge is problematic. Let's take a look at common urges that are associated with each emotion and then what some examples of opposite action might

Emotion	Common Urges	Opposite Action
Anger *(irritated, annoyed, mad, ticked off, frustated, hateful)*	Aggressive words and action	Deep breathing
	Running away from the problem	Walk away
	Avoidance of the problem	Lay down
	Grimmacing	Progressive muscle relaxation
		Half Smile and Willing Hands
		Do something kind for someone/something else in the world

be.

Emotion	Common Urges	Opposite Action
Sadness (bummed, depressed, lonely, unhappy, worthless)	Laying around	Get out of the environment: go for a walk
	Sleeping	Take a shower
	Staying in or putting on pajamas/sweat pants	Exercise
		Call someone
	Hunched shoulders	Watch comedy show, listen to upbeat music
	Slow speech	
	Listening to sad music	

Emotion	Common Urges	Opposite Action
Anxiety	Avoiding the situation	Paced Breathing
(worry, fear, uneasy, uncomfortable, overwhelmed, panic)	Ruminating	Approach the sitiuation (if safe) and take it all in with confidence
	Pacing	
	Freeze in place	Talk openly about fears
	Go silent	Use power posing (confident posture)
		Make eye contact

Meditation as opposite action

Thoughts on meditation are sprinkled throughout this book. I am always hesitant to push people into meditation because it seems to be an intimidating topic. It once was quite intimidating to me as well, yet now it brings such comfort and clarity. When we are immersed in our feelings and don't quite know what to do with them, the idea of sitting still and meditating can seem so overwhelming and can bring about quite a strong sensation of fear! Meditating is the opposite action! I, too, have times where I default to thinking that THIS TIME, I am too anxious to meditate. THIS TIME it won't help. THIS TIME, I can't handle the quiet ….and yet …those times are when I find the greatest clarity. Those times are when I need it most. Those times are when I fall in love with meditation again, and again, and again.

I believe for beginners (and when I am having one of THOSE DAYS), it's easiest to either meditate in a group or use a guided meditation. I encourage you to play around with different apps, videos, websites, and local meditation groups that are available to you. Most major cities have a formal "Zen Center," meditation centers, and/or yoga studios with group meditations.

Meditation will teach you that you are not your emotion. It will show you that you can exist as a strong, stable force (such as a mountain), and you can weather a storm. I love the metaphor of a hurricane to teach meditation. Sometimes when I suggest it to a client, they look at me like I just suggested that they ignore the fact that they are standing in the middle of a hurricane and continue to paint their nails. It's absurd! Why would you ignore a hurricane!? The thing to wrap your head around is that you cannot control life's hurricanes; to do so is like trying to grab onto the debris that is swirling past you at 80 miles per hour. It can kill you! Meditating allows you to honor the fact that you are in a hurricane, we aren't ignoring the truth, while finding the calm eye of the hurricane to rest in and decide on your most effective course of action. Meditation allows you to sit still and say to yourself *"There is a shit-storm swirling around me. I can make things worse, or I can make things better. I need to center myself and decide what to do next to remain effective."* Meditation is also a great tool to keep you healthy in the day-to-day, like ABC PLEASE.

This chapter offers you a plethora of ways to experience and relate to your emotions. Please remember that there is not a one-size-fits-all skill to use in every situation. You must use your own wise mind to determine which course of action, which equation of skills to use in each situation. Keep at it; remember: all things get easier with practice.

Reflect by journaling: How do I typically relate to intense emotions? Is that working for me? What skills from this chapter do I need to work on first? Do I need to lay a firm foundation with any of the PLEASE skills first? In re-visiting the most difficult triggers from the start of this chapter, what skills can I practice when those situations arise again (and again, and again …)? What is my mindset on meditation at this point?

13 HOW DO I KNOW WHERE I AM GOING WRONG?

Ahh troubleshooting ...the bane of our existence sometimes!

- When we feel like we have a semblance of a plan, asking ourselves what to do if the skills do not work can be scary!
- Asking ourselves where we are going wrong can feel threatening as well as insinuating that we (gasp!) are the (or part of the) problem!
- If we are trying to apply solutions and they are not working, sometimes it becomes clear that we are addressing the wrong thing.

At that point, you must do the labor-intensive task of starting over at assessing the situation. DBT® teaches problem solving in a hands-on, relatable fashion. I love teaching this skill because I find that it honors the fact that it is not always that easy to figure out what the problem is or what to do about it! We also have a tool called chain analysis to really start exploring our own patterns, which will shed light on how your thoughts, behaviors, and emotions are connected. With a chain analysis, we can also discover what is reinforcing our thoughts, behaviors, and emotions. The reality is that you are NOT crazy. You do what you do because on some level it works. You picked up this book because on some level you want to learn a new way; let's keep digging in on this topic.

Skill: Problem Solving

Are you living crisis to crisis? Are there particular people, places, times, areas, thoughts that continually trip you up and cause problems? DBT® reminds us first that we ALWAYS have a choice. You always have four choices in every situation.

1. Solve the problem – This is the "no brainer" that we do if we can. It is a choice and merits remembering.

2. Feel better about the problem – You do have a choice in what interpretation you use, which will change how you feel about the problem. The risk here is if you keep trying to convince yourself that "*it's not that bad*" when it (or he, or she, or they) IS that bad and you need to problem solve in a different way. This is a GREAT option if you are a pessimist and tend to see the worst in everything.

3. Tolerate the problem – If you default to this option, you aren't changing much in terms of how you see or relate to it (which changes your emotional attachment to the problem); rather, you are accepting it as a thorn in your side and using distraction whenever it starts to bother you again. This is helpful short-term but not always helpful long-term.

4. Stay miserable/make it worse – I LOVE that we have this choice. The angsty teenager in me needs to be reminded that I can always *say the thing or do the thing or throw the thing or refuse to show up*, etc. I need to mentally walk down that path sometimes to get unstuck from my "*it's not fair*" temper tantrum that I sometimes throw. An example of this could be when you find yourself resenting an obligation to show up somewhere (i.e.: work). Remind yourself that you do not have to go. You could stay home. You might get fired and then you would not have income, but you really do have that choice. Walking down that path can remind you that you do not want to lose your housing, you do want to have money for food and fun; therefore, you will now use strategy #2 and choose to go, but with a different mindset. You might adopt the mental mantra of, "*I'm choosing to go to work so that I can choose to buy the shoes I want.*" which is different and less problematic than, "*I have to go to work, I hate my job, this sucks.*"

Problem solving is NOT always "that easy," and DBT® teaches an additional step by step approach that can walk you through and help you find more creative solutions which will free you from the negative emotions you associate with the problem you have identified. We will walk through the steps below and then I will give you a worksheet for practice.

Step One: Identify and describe the problem –

Using the STOP skill, you need to slow down and assess your state of mind. If you are not in wise mind, you would be better off using other skills to get to wise mind and center yourself before mindfully considering what the problem really is. If you are judging others or the situation, you are not yet in a state of mind to be able to see clearly what the problem is. A big clue that you have identified a solvable problem is that the problem is about you, not the other person/the situation.

Example #1: *The problem is that my dad is inconsiderate.* This is not a problem to work on because you cannot control another person. Blaming or judging another person for your negative emotional experience will not end well. The problem to identify needs to be something within your control. Examples might be: "I chose to attend a family function and had expectations that my dad would respect my request not to discuss my marriage," or "I allowed myself to fall into judgmental thinking related to my dad's choices," or "I called my dad and opened the line of communication that I had decided was unhealthy for me." Any of those can be solved, judging or blaming another person/situation cannot.

Example #2: *The problem is that gas prices rose when I needed gas, and I didn't have enough money, so I ran out of gas on the highway.* Blaming the gas station does not solve the problem. Examples that you can work on might be: "I avoid checking my car's fuel gauge unless the warning light comes on" or "I have not created a budget for my monthly fuel expenses."

Step Two: Check the Facts to be sure it is the correct problem –

Sometimes to check the facts, we need help from another person. This might mean you ask an honest friend or family member, your therapist, or even Google! We need to think rationally and reflect on our own patterns related to the identified problem.

Example #1: *You can check the facts here by asking your therapist and/or close friends if you do have a pattern of expectations related to your dad. You can ask them if you've said you will do anything different in your relationship with him. You can mentally re-play what happened to look for your role and the facts as they were, not as you might exaggerate them to be.*

Example #2: *You could check the facts by Googling fuel price trends to see if they jump randomly or if they only jump on days you fill up. You could reflect on how often you check your car's fuel gauge. You could ask a friend if they have noticed anything about your related choices that seems problematic.*

Step Three: Find your goal for solving the problem –

Try to identify what you would like to see happen in the situation for you to feel less upset (angry, sad, anxious, hurt, etc.) about it. As Stephen Covey says: "Begin with the end in mind." It needs to be simple, achievable, and be a sensical solution. The solution should not be avoidance-based. Using our opposite action skills, we know that we need to approach, not avoid, if we want to decrease our anxiety.

Example #1: *Your goal might be to work on accepting your dad's personality so that it is not as upsetting in the future, it might be to limit time together to once per week in 3 hours or less, or it might be to decrease your own judgments of others/him. Choosing a goal such as moving to a different state might seem like a good choice; however, avoidance of the problem is not a solution that will work.*

Example #2: *Your goal might be to never run out of fuel again, it might be to check your gauge daily and not let it dip under ¼ of a tank, or it might be to reduce blaming others for your mistakes.*

Step Four: Brainstorm solutions –

This is the most fun step in my opinion. In this step, I want you to come up with as many possible solutions as you can. They might seem only partially related to the problem, they might seem outlandish, they might be unattainable; write them all down! What I see happening is that most people can come up with between 5-10 realistic solutions. The problem with this is that for the most part, they are the solutions you have probably already tried. After that, I notice that people tend to use their sense of humor or fantasy thinking, and they come up with some outlandish *"solutions."* These might be things like *"I'll hire a butler"* or *"I'll take a personal jet to India and…."* This is what we did as children, and usually someone squashes our ideas very quickly (and with an attitude of annoyance), but now, we squash our own ideas! I say bring them on and let them flow onto the paper. Once we allow the ridiculous ideas to be put on the list, an amazing thing happens: NEW realistic solutions often bubble up! On the flip side, if we squash our own ideas because they are too silly, our idea pool seems to dry up completely! In this section, we want LOTS of ideas.

Example 1: *DEARMAN dad and ask him to make a change. Avoid him forever. Blame myself. Move out of state. Hire an alien to reprogram him. Go to family therapy. Move out of the country. Pretend nothing happened. Have a baby; they fix everything. Adjust my own expectations. Attend support groups for personal growth.*

Example 2: *Fill my tank every Saturday. Check my fuel level every morning. Set an alarm on my phone to check it. Use gift cards to buy fuel. Get an electric car. Use a jet pack to get to work. Take public transportation. Work on acceptance of price fluctuations. Boycott one brand of fuel. Ask a friend to be my accountability partner. Create a monthly budget.*

Step Five: Choose a solution –

In choosing a solution, we need to ensure that we are still in wise mind so that we can choose an effective one. While it might be fun to try some of the outlandish suggestions, we also need to keep one foot in reality and enact a solution that might work. If a few of the ideas sound good, we can do a pros and cons of them to get more insight.

Example #1: *I will try to adjust my own expectations.*

Example #2: *I will try top off my fuel tank every Saturday and Wednesday.*

Step Six: Take Action –

Remember that there is no "right" answer. You are not married to the first solution you try. We need to stay in a curious-explorer state of mind and try something with little expectation. You may need to create baby steps for your solution, as it is not always going to be a simple solution to enact. This is like long-term accumulate positives from chapter twelve. Sometimes the solution we have identified seems too big or overwhelming. You will need to break it down into smaller step to make it more achievable.

Example #1: *I need support to make this happen, so I will take the following baby steps: read a self-help book on the topic, talk to my therapist about it, journal about it, daily meditation, and seek out a positive support community via my church.*

Example #2: *I will top off my fuel tank on Saturdays and Wednesdays, and I will work on my own judgment of fuel prices by practicing acceptance-based skills.*

Step Seven: Evaluate the results –

Again, it is crucial to remember that we are in a curious state of mind. Do not judge yourself for choosing a solution that did not work or didn't work as well as you had hoped. You do not need to overly inflate yourself for a positive outcome, either (remember that any judging leads to more judging). You can take a moment to revel and feel proud of the accomplishment that you made it this far, whether the outcome was the one you wanted or not.

Example #1: *The self-help book was boring, and I did not get far into it before quitting. I did find it helpful to journal and talk to my therapist. Things are not fixed yet, but I believe I need more time to continue on this path in order to improve my outlook and thus my relationship with him.*

Example #2: *I realized I am not sure if I need fuel once a week or more often. I will first track my fuel consumption for three weeks. Then I will create a monthly budget with fuel included. Finally, I will pick one or two days a week to top off, regardless of the fuel level.*

Step Eight: Reward or Try again –

If you took the time to really work through your problem and come up with creative and wise-minded solutions, you should praise yourself! Recall from our chapter on behaviorism that humans do not tend to make changes unless we are rewarded along the way. If this process was helpful, you need to praise yourself to remember to use the skill next time you encounter a problem! If the solution did not work as well as you'd expected …that's ok! Go back to step five and move through the rest of the process again. Please note that if you try several solutions to no avail, you may need to go all the way back to step one and explore whether you have the correct problem OR you may need to work on acceptance of the situation being out of your control (which is a solution in itself).

Skill: Chain Analysis

The last big skill that you can use, now that you have gotten to the end of the book, is the skill of a behavioral chain analysis. This is an immensely helpful tool in trying to figure out "what the heck is going on"! Sometimes you may feel so trapped in habitual behaviors and processes that you struggle to understand where/how you have gone wrong and/or why you keep doing certain things. Identifying the relationship between your triggers, thoughts, feelings, and actions is essential (and difficult). Often-times, "it all happens so fast" that you are left reeling and unclear on how the situation played out. A behavioral chain analysis (aka "a chain") can help you to slow down and explore the events. After doing several chains on problem behaviors …you will start to find common links and develop a plan to change the outcome! Once your chain is complete, a solution analysis is weaved into each step, which will leave you with numerous ideas on how to intervene. While chains can seem overwhelming at first, they offer a much-needed sense of hope.

The first thing your chain needs is a legend. My suggestion is as follows:

T: Thoughts (this includes judgments, thoughts you had about the situation, etc.)

E: Emotions (I do not use F for Feelings because feelings and sensations can be confused)

S: Sensations (what do you feel in your body/where/how intense)

A: Actions that you took or that happened in the environment

U: Urges (any urge you had, whether you acted on it or not)

I will provide a blank template for a chain, and some example chains on the next pages. First, I need to introduce some words and their definitions:

- The "prompting event" is often known as the trigger and/or the straw that broke the camel's back.
- Your "vulnerabilities" are the straws that were stacking up, your stressors from that day/week.
- Your "target behavior" is the thing that you are trying to stop doing: self-harm, eating disorder behavior, self-judgment, promiscuous behavior, lashing out, using drugs/alcohol, too much screen time, etc. Note: it can be a situation of inaction (i.e.: I've been wanting to speak up for myself and I didn't, I intended to go to the gym, and I didn't, etc.)
- Your "consequences/reinforcers" are what follow the target behavior; this includes the positive experience you gain from having engaged in the target behavior as well as any negative consequences.
- "Solutions" are skills you could try to see if you can alter the outcome of your situation.

The chain should only cover approximately one hour prior to engaging in the target behavior. If you believe your prompting event was more than one hour before …then you're probably identifying it as a vulnerability factor, and you need to dig a little deeper to determine what really set the target behavior in motion. Sometimes we can handle some big stressors (vulnerability factors) and then a smaller issue is what tips the scales. That is ok, and it's good for you to recognize the patterns in yourself. You might struggle to come up with as much detail as the examples have initially; however, with practice, it gets easier to notice and capture the details! Once you complete your chain, in as much detail as possible, you will try to add a solution to as many points as possible. These can be small solutions or large. Typically, the earlier you intervene, the easier it will be and the whole chain could unfold in a completely different (and more effective) way. We will explore solutions more after the chains.

In doing a chain remember to be a curious scientist. You will be able to see more factors in your chain if you do so though the freshest set of eyes possible…a great phrase to think is, "*I wonder if* _____ *is related/important.*" Initially, write it all down! You will not know what's really important until you do several chains on similar events.

Skill Practice: Chain Analysis

Vulnerability Factors:

LEGEND:

T: Thoughts

E: Emotions

S: Sensations

A: Actions

Prompting Event/Trigger:

Target Behavior:

Consequences/Reinforcers:

Example:

Vulnerability Factors: *overslept (feeling rushed), had low-grade headache most of afternoon, annoyed by a post I saw someone made online, generally sensitive to rejection (pertinent in this situation)*

Prompting Event/Trigger:

A: I got a text message from my friend Eliza, cancelling our plans for this evening @ 4pm

S: Sinking feeling, heavy, instant tears stinging

T: I have been looking forward to this all day

E: Disappointment

A: Texting her back, asking why @ 4:05pm

A: She said "something came up"

T: I bet someone asked her to do something more fun. No one likes hanging out with me.

A: finished up at work, took around 20 min. I was generally grouchy and negative the whole time.

U: Eat chocolate, call other people to talk back about Eliza (seeking validation)

A: Stopped at grocery on my way home (coupled with T: I guess I need to figure out food for tonight) @ 4:45pm

A: Strolling through grocery, saw alcohol

U: Drink

T: I deserve this, today sucked

A: Bought a new wine spritzer and frozen dinner

T: This looks yummy, it will cheer me up. I do not care about the food.

A: went home, changed into PJs (at 5pm) and turned-on Netflix

T: fuck it, no one cares about me

U: call my neighbor to come over, she always cheers me up

T: I don't want to bother her, didn't call.

S: heavy

E: very sad, lonely

A: scrolling social media

T: Everyone has friends

S: tears stinging my eyes

Target Behavior: drank too much alcohol (4 drinks between 6-7:30pm)

Consequences/Reinforcers:

S: felt warm, cozy, numb

T: blank

S: tears stopped

E: Calm

A: went to sleep early around 7:30pm

Note: The next morning I felt awful, sluggish, and had a slight headache. I was irritable at work all day. I am mad at myself because I did not get anything done at home, spent too much money on alcohol, and didn't even try any of my skills.

Once you have completed as much of your chain as you can, you need to weave in the solution analysis. If you skip this step, you may feel worse. Solutions always generate hope. A solution analysis is where you go through every identified link on your chain and try to come up with at least one solution/effective change/coping skill/alternate choice which would alter the remainder of the chain (hopefully for the better)! See below for examples; I suggest writing the solutions right on your chain in a brighter color or highlight them so that they stand out.

Chain link:	Proposed Solutions:
Overslept	Create sleep schedule, use alarms, set coffee pot the night before
Headaches	Drink more water, take over-the-counter headache medicine, go for walks as tension is noticed, slow, deep breathing breaks throughout the day
Annoyed by online content	Shut down social media, only check it once per day, practice being non-judgmental, follow more positive content
Sinking feeling	Go for a walk, half-smile, positive self-talk
Texting her back right away	Wait until I feel more centered before texting back, reach out to other people first about general topics to try and regulate myself first
Assuming someone asked her to do something more fun	Check the facts
Being grouchy at work while wrapping up	Opposite action! Half-smile, willing hands, turning the mind
Thinking alcohol will cheer me up	Check the facts, find a replacement treat (i.e.: unique popsicles!)
Thinking "no one cares"	Text a few people to see if they want to hang out tonight or soon, opposite action
Watching Netflix	Engage in a hobby to build mastery or go out with friends/visit a family member to accumulate positives

When doing a solution analysis, I am always amazed by how many solutions I can come up with, in a fairly short amount of time! This generates hope because initially we often think that we had "no choice". Remember: you ALWAYS have a choice! You can use problem solving, revisit the four options for solving any problems, or do a full chain when you find yourself feeling "stuck".

If this book teaches you anything, I hope that it is that you remember that there is always another way. There is always another option. In wise-mind, you make good choices and have great ideas!

You are not stuck …

You are not hopeless …

You ARE capable …

You ARE worthy …

You ARE able to make change!

14 FINAL THOUGHTS

The major take-aways from this book, if I can boil it down to a few points for you, are as follows:

1.   Awareness is key.

You need to be mindful and curious, awake to your realities to discover patterns. Not judging yourself is crucial so that you can really see the patterns in your life, your choices, and interactions.

2.   Motivation is required.

Often when embarking on a journey, you will feel motivated; however, as time goes on, that motivation can wax and wane. When this happens, do not despair! It is normal and natural. Slow down and remind yourself why you want things to improve. Take a break, and that motivation will return in time! I have found that when motivation is low, you need to keep trudging (slowly) in the initial (wise-minded) direction, so that when motivation returns you won't have to make up lost ground.

10

Intense emotions. Unable to problem solve or think clearly.

Crisis zone – Use distress tolerance skills to avoid making things worse.

Consider TIPP for the most extreme emotions, review your pros and cons to stay motivated, and IMPROVE/Self-Soothe/ACCEPT to distract yourself until you regulate enough to enter the emotion zone below.

Emotions are evident and/or somewhat problematic. You CAN cope.

Emotion zone - Use emotion regulation skills

Consider opposite action for the most intense emotions you can handle, problem solving for mid-level emotions, and ABC PLEASE when you first notice them rising to insulate yourself.

Only attempt interpersonal effectiveness (communication skills) when at 50% intensity or lower.

Chill zone – Use mindfulness skills to stay here!

0

Skill reference guide:

		Mindfulness
		Wise Mind
	What Skills	**Observe:** just notice (urge surfing) -You are not your urge; stay on top of it
		Describe: put words on
		Participate: enter the experience-Letting yourself go; get lost in something
	How Skills	**One mindfully:** in the moment
		Non-judgmentally: just the facts, don't judge judging
		Effectively: focus on what works, do what needs to be done
Interpersonal Effectiveness		**Prioritize** among interpersonal goals
		Consider **options** for **intensity**
	3 goals of interpersonal effectiveness	**Objectives** effectiveness: **DEAR MAN**
		Relationship Effectiveness: **GIVE**
		Self-respect Effectiveness: **FAST**
Emotion Regulation		**Check the Facts** are your emotions/actions justified by the situation
		Problem Solve

ABC	**A**ccumulate positives: Do pleasant things that are possible now
PLEASE	**B**uild mastery: Do things that make you feel competent and effective
	Cope Ahead: Rehearse the plan ahead of time
	Take care of **P**hysical illness
	Balanced **E**ating
	Avoid alcohol / mood altering drugs
	Balanced **S**leeping
	Balanced **E**xercise
	Let go of emotional Suffering: Experience my emotion as a wave

Distress Tolerance		**STOP** Skill
		TIPP
		Pros / cons
	Distract Skills ACCCEPTS	**A**ctivities
		Contribution (do something for others)
		Comparison / Count blessings (compare to past self/situations)
		Opposite **E**motions (acting opposite your emotion urge)
		Pushing away (put on a shelf & lock it away ...will come back to it)
		Thoughts (think about something more pleasant)
		Sensations (seek to stimulate ...exercise, ice, cold shower, strong taste/smell)
		Self-soothe with 5 senses
	IMPROVE the moment	**I**magery (send mind to another place)
		Meaning (find something meaningful in the moment)
		Prayer (or mantra)
		Relaxation
		One thing in the moment
		Vacation (figuratively or literally)
		Self - **E**ncouragement

	Acceptance Skills	**Observe the breath**
		Half-smile/ Willing Hands
		Radical acceptance, turning the mind (accept & bring yourself back)
		Willingness
	Middle	**Dialectics**
	Path	**Validation**
	Skills	**Behaviorism to change Behavior**

Post Test: Self-Assessment - Who are you now?

As you finish the work presented in this book, let's take a snapshot of who you are now; you can compare this to your pre-test and see where you have made the most change. This can also show you where you would like to do a bit more work. Remember …no one is perfect, and our work here is never truly finished.

Name: _____ Age: _____

Occupation: _____

How would you rate your ability to tolerate urges in the areas mentioned below, on a scale of 0-5 (0= no control, 3 = moderate control and 5 = complete control)?

Financial urges: Self-harm urges:

Time management urges: Peer-pressure urges:

Anger urges: Sad urges:

Anxiety urges: Food related urges:

Substance use urges:

I believe my biggest strengths are:

I believe I need to grow/change in the following areas:

I am satisfied with these areas of my life:

I am dissatisfied with these areas of my life:

References

• Linehan, M. (1993). Cognitive-behavioral treatment of borderline personality disorder. New York, New York: The Guilford Press

• Linehan, M. (2015). DBT skills training handouts and worksheets (Second ed.). New York, New York: The Guilford Press.

• Goodman, M., Carpenter, D., Tang, C., Goldstein, K., Avedon, J., Fernandez, N., . . . Hazlett, E. (2014). Dialectical behavior therapy alters emotion regulation and amygdala activity in patients with borderline personality disorder. doi: 10.1016/j.jpsychires.2014.06.020

• Pryor, K. (1999). Don't Shoot The Dog!: The New Art of Teaching and Training (Rev. ed.). New York, New York: Bantam Books.

• Shenk, C., & Fruzzetti, A. (2011). The Impact of Validating and Invalidating Responses on Emotional Reactivity. Journal of Social and Clinical Psychology, 30(2), 163-183.

• Levenson, R., Carstensen, L., & Gottman, J. (1994). Influence of age and gender on affect, physiology, and their interrelations: A study of long-term marriages. Journal of Personality and Social Psychology, 67, 56-68.

• Carre, S., Mittmann, A., Woodin, E., Tabares, A., & Yoshimoto, D. (2005). Anger Dysregulation, Depressive Symptoms, and Health in Married Women and Men. Nursing Research, 54, 184-192.

• Levenson, R., Carstensen, L., & Gottman, J. (1994). Influence of age and gender on affect, physiology, and their interrelations: A study of long-term marriages. Journal of Personality and Social Psychology, 67, 56-68.

• Gottman, J., & Levenson, R. (2002). A Two-Factor Model for Predicting When a Couple Will Divorce: Exploratory Analyses Using 14-Year Longitudinal Data*. Family Process, 41, 83-96.

• Frank, M., & Ekman, P. (1996). Physiological Effects of the Smile. Directions in Psychiatry, 16(25). Retrieved April 16, 2018, from https://1ammce38pkj41n8xkp1iocwe-wpengine.netdna-ssl.com/wp-content/uploads/2013/07/Physiological-Effects-Of-The-Smile.pdf.

• Carney, D., Cuddy, A., & Yapp, A. (2010). Power Posing: Brief Nonverbal Displays Affect Neuroendocrine Levels and Risk Tolerance.

Association for Psychological Science, 21(10), 1363-1368.
doi:10.1177/0956797610383437

• Seligman, M. E. P. (1975). Helplessness: On Depression, Development, and Death. San Francisco: W. H. Freeman. ISBN 0-7167-2328-X.

• Jewell, L. (2017). Wire your brain for confidence: The science of conquering self-doubt. Toronto, Canada: Famous Warrior Press.

• Vanderkam, Laura. (October, 2016). How to Gain Control of Your Free Time Retrieved from https://www.ted.com/talks/laura_vanderkam_how_to_gain_control_of_your_free_time.

• Koulivand, P., Ghadiri, M., & Gorji, A. (2013). Lavender and the Nervous System. Evid Based Complement Alternat Medicine. doi:10.1155/2013/681304

• Perry, N., & Perry, E. (2006). Aromatherapy in the Management of Psychiatric Disorders. CNS Drugs, 20(4), 257-280. doi:10.2165/00023210-200620040-00001

• Spark, N. T. (2006). Whatever can go wrong, will go wrong: A history of Murphys Law. Place of publication not identified: Publisher not identified.

• Instagram 'worst for young mental health'. (2017, May 19). Retrieved May 7, 2018, from http://www.bbc.com/news/health-39955295

• Squires, D. (2016, October 24). Everything You Always Wanted to Know About Social Media: History and Different Types of Social Media. Retrieved May 8, 2018, from http://scalar.usc.edu/works/everything-you-always-wanted-to-know-about-social-media-but-were-too-afraid-to-ask/history-and-different-types-of-social-media

• Kent C. Berridge and Terry E. Robinson, What is the role of dopamine in reward: hedonic impact, reward learning, or incentive salience?: Brain Research Reviews, 28, 1998. 309–369.

• Sidani, J., et al, "The Association between Social Media Use and Eating Concerns among US Young Adults," Journal of the Academy of Nutrition and Dietetics, September (2016), Volume 116, Issue 9: Pages

1465–1472.

• Levenson, JC, et al, "Social Media Use Before Bed and Sleep Disturbance Among Young Adults in the United States: A Nationally Representative Study," Sleep, 2017 Sep 1;40(9).

• Sherman, Lauren, et al, "The Power of the Like in Adolescence: Effects of Peer Influence on Neural and Behavioral Responses to Social Media," Psychological Science, May (2016), Vol 27, Issue 7.

• Smith, P. C., & Curnow, R. (1966). "Arousal hypothesis" and the effects of music on purchasing behavior. Journal of Applied Psychology, 50(3), 255-256.

• Milliman, R. E. (1986). The Influence of Background Music on the Behavior of Restaurant Patrons. Journal of Consumer Research, 13(2), 286. doi:10.1086/209068

• Caldwell, C., & Hibbert, S. (1999). Play That One Again: The Effect of Music Tempo on Consumer Behaviour in a Restaurant. European Advances in Consumer Research, 4, 58-62. Retrieved July 31, 2018, from https://www.acrwebsite.org/search/view-conference-proceedings.aspx?Id=11116.

• Jewell, L. (2017). Wire your brain for confidence: The science of conquering self-doubt. Toronto, Canada: Famous Warrior Press.

• Brown, B. (2015). Daring Greatly: How the Courage to be Vulnerable Transforms the Way We Live, Love, Parent, and Lead. London, England: Penguin Books.

• Lim, N. (june 2016). Cultural differences in emotion: Differences in emotional arousal level between the East and the West. Ntegrative Medicine Research, 5(2), 105-109. doi:10.3726/978-3-653-01466-2/12

• Emory Health Sciences. (2014, November 18). High-fructose diet in adolescence may exacerbate depressive-like behavior. ScienceDaily. Retrieved November 3, 2019 from www.sciencedaily.com/releases/2014/11/141118141852.htm

• Agrawal, R., & Gomez-Pinilla, F. (2012). 'Metabolic syndrome' in the brain: deficiency in omega-3 fatty acid exacerbates dysfunctions in insulin receptor signalling and cognition. The Journal of Physiology, 590(10), 2485–2499.

• Suicide Prevention. (n.d.). Retrieved November 11, 2019, from https://www.nimh.nih.gov/health/topics/suicide-prevention/index.shtml.

• Shallcross, L. J., & Davies, D. S. C. (2014). Antibiotic overuse: a key driver of antimicrobial resistance. British Journal of General Practice, 64(629), 604–605. doi: 10.3399/bjgp14x682561

• Do Americans Watch More DVR'd Commercials Than You Think. (2012, December 21). Retrieved from https://www.nielsen.com/us/en/insights/article/2010/do-americans-watch-more-dvrd-commercials-than-you-think/.

• National Highway Traffic Safety Administration. Traffic Safety Facts Research Notes 2016: Distracted Driving.S. Department of Transportation, Washington, DC: NHTSA; 2015. Available at https://crashstats.nhtsa.dot.gov/Api/Public/ViewPublication/812517e xternal icon. Accessed 25 March 2019

• Bacon, L., & Aphramor, L. (2011, January 24). Weight science: evaluating the evidence for a paradigm shift. Retrieved from https://www.ncbi.nlm.nih.gov/pmc/articles/PMC3041737/.

• Best-Sellers Initially Rejected. (n.d.). Retrieved November 11, 2019, from http://www.litrejections.com/best-sellers-initially-rejected/.

• Kaimal, D., Sajja, R. T., & Sasangohar, F. (2017). Investigating the Effects of Social Media Usage on Sleep Quality. Proceedings of the Human Factors and Ergonomics Society Annual Meeting, 61(1), 1327–1330. doi: 10.1177/1541931213601814

• Kaneita, Y., Ohida, T., Osaki, Y., Tanihata, T., Minowa, M., Suzuki, K., … Hayashi, K. (2007). Association Between Mental Health Status and Sleep Status Among Adolescents in Japan. The Journal of Clinical Psychiatry, 68(09), 1426–1435. doi: 10.4088/jcp.v68n0916

• Anderson, K., & Bradley. (2013). Sleep disturbance in mental health problems and neurodegenerative disease. Nature and Science of Sleep, 61. doi: 10.2147/nss.s34842

• Attwood, A. S., & Munafò, M. R. (2014). Effects of acute alcohol consumption and processing of emotion in faces: Implications for understanding alcohol-related aggression. Journal of Psychopharmacology, 28(8), 719–732. doi: 10.1177/0269881114536476

• University of Granada. (2011, February 3). Drug-abusers have difficulty to recognize negative emotions as wrath, fear and sadness, study finds. ScienceDaily. Retrieved November 10, 2019 from www.sciencedaily.com/releases/2011/02/110203082521.htm

• María José Fernández-Serrano, Óscar Lozano, Miguel Pérez-García, Antonio Verdejo-García. Impact of severity of drug use on discrete emotions recognition in polysubstance abusers. Drug and Alcohol Dependence, 2010; 109 (1-3): 57 DOI: 10.1016/j.drugalcdep.2009.12.007

• María José Fernández-Serrano, Miguel Pérez-García, José C. Perales, Antonio Verdejo-García. Prevalence of executive dysfunction in cocaine, heroin and alcohol users enrolled in therapeutic communities. European Journal of Pharmacology, 2010; 626 (1): 104 DOI: 10.1016/j.ejphar.2009.10.019

• Chekroud SR, Gueorguieva R, Zheutlin AB, Paulus M, Krumholz HM, Krystal JH, Chekroud AM. Association between physical exercise and mental health in 1·2 million individuals in the USA between 2011 and 2015: a cross-sectional study. Lancet Psychiatry. 2018;5(9):739-746. doi: 10.1016/S2215-0366(18)30227-X. Epub 2018 Aug 8

• Association between physical exercise and mental health in ... (2018, September 1). Retrieved from https://www.thelancet.com/journals/lanpsy/article/PIIS2215-0366(18)30227-X/fulltext.

• Anderson E, Shivakumar G Effects of Exercise and Physical Activity on Anxiety. Front Psychiatry. 2013;4:27. Available at: https://www.ncbi.nlm.nih.gov/pmc/articles/PMC3632802/ Accessed Feb. 1, 2019

Made in the USA
Monee, IL
12 May 2022

96270765R00146